TOUCHED
by the
DRAGON'S BREATH

Conversations at Colliding Rivers

MICHAEL HARRINGTON

Susan Creek Books
Wilsonville, Oregon

Touched by the Dragon's Breath

Conversations at Colliding Rivers

Copyright © 2003 Michael Harrington
First Edition—2005
Fourth Printing—2009

Cover design by Aimee Genter
Cover verse adapted from a saying by Robert Ghost Wolf
Initial edit by Judith Irwin
Final edit by Leslie Dyer
Typesetting by Brenda Evans

ISBN #: 978-0-9748716-0-8
Library of Congress #: 2005924411

Besides references, the "Notes" section of this book contains important facts, supplemental information, and additional resources.

The author does not dispense medical advice nor prescribe medical treatment for physical, mental, or emotional imbalances. The information presented here—as with any outside information—should be viewed as seed material for contemplation only.

Susan Creek Books
29030 SW Town Center Loop E.
Suite 202-250
Wilsonville, OR 97070
(503) 516-1106
www.SusanCreek.com

Printed in the U.S.A. by
Morris Publishing
3212 East Highway 30
Kearney, NE 68847
1-800-650-7888

DEDICATION

To Gene

To the White Fire Beings

TABLE OF CONTENTS

PART I

ELEVENTH HOUR ON THE COSMIC CLOCK

PART II

A RETURN TO SELF-KNOWLEDGE

PART III

CROSSING THE GOLDEN THRESHOLD

LIST OF ILLUSTRATIONS

PREFACE

In the fall of 1987 my conversations with John Redstone at Colliding Rivers had just begun. But the world as I had known it was ending. The *Golden Threshold of 2012* seemed an eternity away. Yet, with the passing of the Harmonic Convergence, the midpoint of the 50-year Overlap Zone between the Piscean Age and the Age of Aquarius, Earth's 25-year march toward ascension was now underway.

John Redstone understood the significance of this event and unselfishly shared his insights about the changes ahead: the balancing of the global seedbed, the Magnetic Shift, Zero Point, and the four major cycles that will end in 2012. He was also familiar with the Photon Belt, a spectacular band of multi-dimensional light that St. Germain had called the "Golden Nebula." In esoteric circles it is known as the *Dragon's Breath*.

From our many discussions, I learned why Tibetans and indigenous people throughout the world look forward to the Mayan end-date of December 21, 2012 A.D., and why some consider it the end of time. I learned why the sun will indeed rise in both the east and west on the same day, as Native American prophecy suggests, and why, despite tough times ahead, the future is bright. I also learned why those holding power fear the coming Golden Age...and why today's children are the harbingers of a new, transcendental consciousness.

John Redstone, the man I affectionately called "the Chief," received his information directly from contemplation. He called it "self-knowledge." To those who choose to read this book, be forewarned. Much of what he shared in our Sunday conversations is contrary to conventional teachings on science, religion, and history; most notably, the truth about who we are, why we're here, and where we're going.

My friend and mentor left this world in the spring of 2001, coincidentally the same month that I finished the first draft of this book. Much of the information in *Touched by the Dragon's Breath* can be attributed to the Chief, including the "Golden Formula," a template for upgrading the *Belief System*. In a way, this is his parting gift, his message of hope to a world poised on the threshold of a great transformation. I am grateful for the opportunity to share these principles and insights that have helped me so much.

(NOTE: Chapter 10 contains additional information about 2012 and the Photon Belt from a variety of sources. It is meant to stand alone, and may be read first or in sequence.)

– Michael Harrington
August 2003

INTRODUCTION

The Mayan calendar ends on December 21, 2012 A.D. While this will not mark the extinction of life on this planet, as some fear, it will bring sweeping changes. In the summer of 1987 we first entered a band of multi-dimensional light known as the "Photon Belt."[1] When the full intensity of this electromagnetic band of light arrives around 2012, great changes will occur. Stories alluding to the end of physical time and Zero Point can be traced to this date.

The excitement and awe surrounding 2012 is further heightened by the synchronous ending of four major cycles. With our entrance into Aquarius, the 2,160-year cycle of the Piscean Age is coming to a close. At the same time, Earth's 26,000-year Precession of the Equinoxes—a Mayan Great Cycle—finds completion. Furthermore, according to both the Aztec and Mayan cosmologies, 2012 is the end-point of a 104,000-year cycle composed of four Great Cycles. But most astounding of all is the completion of our solar system's 225-million-year Galactic Orbit, also slated for 2012![2]

The Tibetans look forward to the arrival of 2012 with great anticipation, as well. Their calendar, the *Kalachakra,* contains a prophecy that 860 years after its introduction into Tibet, which happened in 1127, the conditions would be fulfilled for a twenty-five year period that would culminate in the appearance of a sacred Tibetan spiritual city—860 years after 1127 is 1987, the year of the Harmonic Convergence. Twenty-five years after that is 2012![3]

As the winter solstice of 2012 draws nigh, humanity stands poised on the greatest of thresholds. Earth is entering the gateway to a new reality. We are now in the overlap zone between the Piscean Age and the Age of Aquarius. It is a time of preparation. Life is speeding up as third-dimensional energy diminishes, and fourth-dimensional energy bombards the planet both from within and without.

As we enter the Age of Aquarius, the negative influences that have darkened this era will gradually disappear, as those with evil intent leave the planet one by one. And they will not have the opportunity to be reborn on Earth again, as, in its higher state, it will no longer tolerate vibrations of hate, violence, and subjugation. Harmony, longevity, telepathic communication, and manifestation through thought will become commonplace in the coming cycle.

With Earth's cosmic initiation now fully underway, I look around in disbelief. Instead of preparing for this monumental change, few people seem interested in truly bettering their lives, let alone gearing up for a dimensional shift. Could it be they don't know what lies ahead, or perhaps how to prepare? Why else would intelligent people so readily accept the present Orwellian version of reality?

It has long been known that if man ever started thinking for himself he could no longer be controlled. This is why we are inundated with mindless sitcoms, game shows, trivia, and endless distractions. For centuries, knowledge of who we are and how we create our reality has been carefully removed from the public arena.

If our present view of reality is a programmed model designed to keep us in mental bondage, then how do we go about changing it? The answer is simple —we recover the knowledge that has been withheld. Besides examining the Photon Belt and dimensional shift, our return to self-knowledge is the primary focus of this book.

This hidden knowledge includes who we are, why we're here, and how we create our reality by setting "still ideas" in motion through imagination and thought. Reading the works of others, no matter how uplifting, cannot instill wisdom or change one thing in our lives. Our own electronic keynote must be placed on the images through imagination before success can be enjoyed. Cosmic law states: "Whatever the mind of man can *imagine* must become reality!"[4]

This hidden knowledge also includes the light wave of creation, the true purpose of mind, the *Golden Thread* that connects all life (sometimes called Spirit, or the Holy Spirit), and the Belief System, also called the "Seedbed."

At every turn, outside forces have manipulated us with guilt and fear. It is no wonder we are addicted, depressed, and enslaved. But take heart, great things await: self-knowledge, happiness, and freedom. There is a light at the end of the tunnel...and that light is the Golden Age!

PART I

ELEVENTH HOUR ON THE COSMIC CLOCK

THE DRAGON'S BREATH
AND THE VALLEY OF MAN

My introduction to 2012 came in 1987, the year of the Harmonic Convergence. (See details in Chapter 2.) I was very naïve. I had no idea that 2012 is one of many "closely guarded secrets" of those who control the power strings of this planet. I hadn't a clue what was coming, much less, how to prepare. Looking back, my life was kin to a flea living contentedly on a runaway dog.

I was relatively happy in my sleepy contentment. I had a red sports car, a steady girlfriend, a decent-paying job, and several friends who wanted better cars, better jobs, and, for the most part, better relationships. While I wanted to improve my life, as well, my inner voice urged me to look beyond the American Dream for my answer.

If there is a reward for living an unorthodox life, it is a greater understanding of reality. But there is also a down side. For instance, there is little joy in finding out that many things we've been taught in school are wrong. In fact, they are utterly false—and not by accident. They are false by design. Organized religion plays an equally sordid role. At this juncture in history every facet of society has been tainted by an agenda of control.

Although fascinating, a study of this agenda and those working behind the scenes to establish a one-world government is beyond the scope of this treatise.[1] For those interested, however, Dr. John Coleman is considered a leading authority on the dark side of globalization. David Icke is another. In *The Biggest Secret* he writes: "Most people will never accept the truth because it is simply too fantastic to be believed."[2] Only by questioning everything, while knowing with absolute certainty that we hold the power to figure things out on our own, can we find the truth.

The first step toward truth, and the freedom it brings, is generally *a desire to better one's life.* The rest of the journey unfolds one step at a time through *understanding.* But sometimes life blesses us with a wake-up call.

Honolulu, Hawaii, 1977

While living in Hawaii, prior to my startling revelation in Tibet ten years later, I had one of those life-changing moments of awakening. Just before lunch I paddled out for one last ride on a surfboard I'd rented from a stand in front of the Royal Hawaiian Hotel in Waikiki. Instead of resting after the tiresome swim out, I took my place at the end of a row of locals.

A glance over my shoulder in the direction of the open sea confirmed what the other surfers already knew. A big wave was building. I paddled ahead furiously, catching the wave along with the locals. I was on top of the world. My feeling of exhilaration vanished, however, when I tumbled off the back of my board. As I bobbed up and down in the tropical surf, I watched the other riders cruise in to shore fifty yards away. I could see my own board floating in their midst. Heaving a weary sigh, I started the long swim back. It took only a moment to realize my terrible predicament.

My arms felt like lead. I swam five difficult yards, then went under. I called out, but the pounding surf drowned my cries for help. Again I went under. Only this time when I surfaced I popped right out of my body!

What a startling experience. I was simply a viewpoint. With heightened clarity and surprising calmness, I surveyed my grim situation from a vantage point about three feet above my left shoulder. I felt no fear, nor was there a sense of desperation or urgency. Mostly, I was mesmerized by the variety of bright colors—the swimsuits, the towels, the flamingo pink face of the Royal Hawaiian Hotel. My own towel was spread out in front of the Outrigger next door. "Will I ever lie on it again?" I wondered without concern. Laughing children splashed in the shallow water near the edge of the surf. An indescribable feeling of joy permeated the atmosphere.

There was no perception of time, nor was I particularly attached to the outcome of the drama. I was merely an observer. In fact, as I reveled in this remarkable new freedom, the probability that I would permanently leave the body within the next few minutes seemed far less important than fully processing my new insight—that I existed independent of the body as a spiritual being.

My second insight was as unexpected as the first. As suddenly as I'd left my body, I returned. Another huge wave towered above me. In that moment my heart sank as I faced the inevitable. There was no way out. Only then did it occur to me to ask the Divine for help. I was barely able to whisper a quick, impassioned plea.

As the wave crashed over me I threw out my arms in desperation. A dull thud sent vibrations reverberating up my right arm. I'd hit a board. I held to it with all my strength as I drifted gently toward shore. I was too weak to pull myself on top so I clung to it thankfully, resting my head on its surface. A warm wave of relief flooded through me as my toes finally touched sand. Slowly I opened my eyes and looked around. How could I thank the board's owner?

But no one appeared to be searching for a missing board. With growing perplexity I scanned the beach, this time in a 360-degree sweep. Then I happened to glance down at the number painted on the rented board. I stared at the number "15" in stunned disbelief. This was the same board I had rented only four hours earlier!

That night I posed for a picture with some friends from the mainland on a narrow *lanai* overlooking Waikiki. I was the one with the biggest smile. When the prints came back I noticed something unusual. Above my right shoulder, where a distant light had refracted in the camera lens, shone a blue-white light in the form of a star. I took this as confirmation of Divine Intervention.

I came away from my near-death experience in the Waikiki surf with two powerful insights: a knowingness that I was more than a physical body, and, that help was available for the asking.

For those who have never had this kind of experience, you can see and think with great clarity while outside the body. Some call the viewpoint "Soul." I learned to think of it as "the real me." Whatever label you put on it, you come away knowing that *you are*, and that *you always will be*. There is a certainty to this knowledge, as well, because you have experienced it firsthand. It is "self-knowledge."

In the months that followed I reveled in a new appreciation for life. A growing thirst for knowledge was a by-product of this shift in consciousness. Almost daily I would follow the Ala Wai Canal past row after row of towering condominiums to my sanctuary, the Honolulu Public Library.

One day while browsing through their small metaphysical section I came across an interesting passage. It was a Native American prophecy that told of a dynamic wave of energy traveling through space. When the Earth passed through this wave, the passage stated, great changes would occur. This great transformation would be preceded by a time of purification.

The next morning I returned to re-read the material and to photocopy the passage. I looked everywhere for the book. After an hour of searching, I turned to the librarian in utter frustration. Together we combed the section again, but since I had rifled through dozens of books the day before, I had no recollection of the title. Our search ended in failure.

Of all the books on prophecy I've read and forgotten over the years, it's curious how that particular passage stuck. Perhaps my mind connected the ocean waves in my near-death experience with the "great wave" traveling through space. At any rate, I've never come across the passage anywhere else, which makes me wonder if I only dreamed about it after visiting the library that day.

In addition to prophecy, books on the out-of-the-body state caught my attention. In particular, Paul Twitchell's writings on *Soul Travel* gave specific contemplative exercises for leaving the physical body at will.[3] While I had little conscious success, I would often become "the viewpoint" while drifting off to sleep.

Something else in Twitchell's writings jumped out at me. He stated that the highest state of divine consciousness would often appear as a *blue star* to those in need.[4]

I began spending at least half an hour each evening in contemplation. Just before bedtime I would lie on my back and focus my attention on the spiritual eye. I would mock up a picture of a sunset over the ocean and try to shift all my attention there. Generally I would place myself (as the viewpoint) on a sand dune overlooking the surf. The images were similar to ones you might view in your mind's eye if you had recently been to the beach and were remembering a particular scene.

One night, when I was very relaxed, I noticed that the exercise had moved beyond simple imagination. I first heard seagulls, then waves crashing upon the beach. A few hundred yards out I detected a sailboat with a multi-colored sail. A sailboat had never been part of my mockups. The scene didn't last long; I was so relaxed and undisciplined that I drifted off to sleep. But this small success inspired me to continue.

This 1977 adventure was not my first trip to Hawaii. I had always been attracted to the ancient land, once known as Lemuria in antediluvian times. According to the Naacal writings, reported to be the first known written records of man, its 64,000,000 inhabitants had developed one of the greatest civilizations known to earth. Initially called "MU," Lemuria had colonized much of the world prior to its final destruction by earthquakes and tidal waves more than twelve thousand years ago.[5] The numerous islands dotting the Pacific remain to testify to the continent's beauty, secretly known to some as the "Sunken Garden."

It is claimed that the elders of Lemuria, known as the "Thirteenth School," moved their headquarters to an uninhabited plateau in central Asia prior to the cataclysm. In that region we now call Tibet, they reportedly established a library and school known as "The Great White Brotherhood."[6]

Lemurian masters also set up schools of arcane wisdom in other parts of the world to preserve their scientific and spiritual knowledge. Prior to the cataclysm, the Golden Sun Disc of MU was taken from the great Temple of Divine Light in Lemuria to Peru, where it was guarded by Incan High Priests in a remote monastery high in the Andes Mountains.[7]

James Churchward, author of *The Lost Continent of MU*, claimed that most of Earth's languages could be traced to the symbolic language of MU. Through his knowledge of this language, Churchward was able to uncover numerous tributes to the memory of Lemuria scattered throughout the world. The hieroglyphic title of *The Egyptian Book of the Dead,* for example, literally means "MU has gone forth from the day." Every chapter in the *Book of the Dead* either directly or indirectly refers to MU. Another record, inscribed on a temple wall in the Yucatan reads, "This edifice is a commemorative monument dedicated to the memory of MU—the lands of the West, the birthplace of our sacred mysteries."[8]

I found the most fascinating tribute to be the Greek alphabet. According to Churchward, the letters of the Greek alphabet took shape from a *Cara Maya* (an ancient language) epic memorial to those who lost their lives at the destruction of MU.[9]

One evening I discovered the reason for my interest in the ancient land. After dinner I retreated to a quiet corner to relax and practice my exercises. Forty minutes passed without incident. I was about to quit when something peculiar happened. I found myself climbing down a vertical, metal ladder. Mentally I counted each step as I descended in the darkness. I got the impression that by counting each step I was symbolically going back in time.

The fiftieth one was different. There was sand beneath my feet. I wore new leather sandals that tied around my ankles. Fifty-eight, fifty-nine, sixty... and an immaculate white toga, bound at the waist with a braided gold belt.

My hair was light brown, like my close-cropped beard. I stood six feet in height, self-assured and proud. My eyes mirrored the blue of the Lemurian surf, different than the others, whose eyes were dark brown. Sixty-seven, sixty-eight, sixty-nine... a man of slender build sat cross-legged beneath a palm tree in front of me, to my right. He acknowledged my presence. Had he called my name? Seventy... I stopped.

The man gazed up intently through piercing brown eyes. His attire was similar—tan sandals and a light blue toga. A tan cord crossed diagonally over the right shoulder of his garment after securing the waist. He sat with his back to the orange-gold setting sun. An atmosphere of peace pervaded the area.

I rested my left arm on top of a marble bench while shielding my eyes with my right. There was no one else within a hundred yards. Less than fifty feet away a small sailboat was tethered at the water's edge, its hull laden with provisions enough for a long voyage. The golden light glistening upon the water reminded me of a river flowing to the sun.

Again the man spoke. "The River of God flows from the heart of every creature." It was an unusual thing to say to a total stranger, I thought. I turned my attention to the water. Waves were breaking on the beach nearby, but with such gentleness I could barely hear them. I gazed out upon the river of light flowing toward the sun, now only a half-disc shimmering above the horizon.

The man motioned toward the sea. "Would you like to know where the Golden River ends?" he asked. I smiled politely, but turned away without answering. I hadn't understood what he had meant. The scene faded to a hazy darkness. I came out of my contemplation and went for a walk along the beach to collect my thoughts. A chill swept through me. The sun had set... seventy thousand years before!

Chang Tang Plateau, Tibet

In 1987, ten years after my near-death experience in Hawaii, I had another startling revelation. This one pointed to the future, however, rather than the past. Late one night while reclining on my bed, I closed my eyes and took a few deep breaths to relax the body.

About half an hour into the contemplation I became aware of a dancing light flickering ever so dimly in the darkness of my inner vision. I concentrated all my attention on the light. Even though the images were sketchy, a campfire gradually emerged from the shadows and came into focus. Behind the golden-orange flames, a solid man in a dark-colored robe was seated in lotus fashion, his hands folded in his lap. Keen brown eyes flashed a kind welcome.

Cold—dampness—green nettles—the strong smell of animals. A quick glance around revealed a tiny cave. To my left, a heavy wooden door reinforced with metal slats secured the entrance. Sparse nettles encircled a solitary pool of water to my right. The pungent smell came from a dirty yak hide that cushioned the hard ground beneath me. A stack of dried yak dung chips supplied fuel for the fire. Where is this place? I wondered. Surprisingly, the word "Tibet" rolled through my mind. I tried again. Why am I here? This time no answer.

Evidently satisfied that I was now adequately acclimated, the man rose to his feet. I guessed his age to be in the late seventies, his height about six-feet four. With growing curiosity I followed the man in silence toward the massive door. Rusty hinges responded with a loud creak. The door swung open revealing an awe-inspiring view. Perhaps half a dozen mountain ranges, one behind the next, rolled majestically toward a purple horizon. It was twilight in the Himalayas!

I stepped out onto a narrow trail that wound its way steeply upward toward snow-capped peaks shrouded in clouds. It rose from the valley floor below, an inhospitable, desolate plain. Never before had I seen such a lonely, lifeless place.

Following my gaze, the man spoke for the first time. "The Chang Tang Plateau," he stated. "It is a symbol of man's struggle for liberation. Some call it 'the Valley of Pain and Disillusionment,' others, 'the Wasteland of God'—but it is not God's doing. More aptly it could be called 'the Valley of Man,' because man has created it. For centuries he has misunderstood the mechanics of creation. He has been misled...but this does not excuse him from responsibility."

We walked fifteen yards up the rocky trail. "Let's sit down and wait," he said, in a tone resonating with familiarity. Ten minutes passed—then ten more. Only the barely-audible sound of my breathing interrupted the stillness. A gentle wind sprang up from the mountain at our backs. I was about to ask what we were waiting for when I noticed a high-pitched hum coming from the wind. It grew louder as the velocity increased. From behind this sound another arose: the faint, haunting melody of distant bagpipes. Now the musical wind was brushing my companion's flowing grey hair forward, and tugging mischievously at the edges of my woolen robe.

Then the playful, biting wind changed again. It howled like a wounded animal pushing its way roughly down the mountain with growing determination. I tucked my chin to my chest, bracing myself against the roaring gusts...and still the tempest escalated. I turned to speak, but a raised hand called for silence.

"There!" the man shouted, pointing toward the horizon with childlike anticipation. "Look, there." His eyes danced with joy. "Behold, the Dragon's Breath! It's coming. It's coming!"

In the distance I saw a golden wave of light, so far away that it was hardly more than a line etched upon the purple horizon. Yet it pulsed with life, rising and falling in subtle undulations. I turned to my companion for an explanation, but none was forthcoming.

Suddenly the wind stopped. It didn't just die down. It stopped abruptly. There was an absolute stillness in the air. In that same moment, my Himalayan cat came in from her nightly mouse-hunting expedition on the other side of the globe. The gentle shake of the bed brought me back instantly.

I revisited the experience again and again in the months that followed, trying to understand its meaning and to place where I'd seen the man in the cave. Interpreting the experience as a dream, I surmised that life-altering changes loomed ahead. Often wind from the mountain symbolizes "the wind of change." And the barren plain—the Valley of Pain and Disillusionment—tied to man's reckless creation of his world, something to be corrected.

Finally the identity of the stranger in the cave hit me. He was an acquaintance I'd met in Oregon many years before. The subtle nature of the inner experience and the passage of seventeen years had made recognition difficult. But that wondrous wave of light, the Dragon's Breath, remained a total mystery.

*   *   *

Each morning I wake
to a heart of fire,
touched by the splendor
of the Dragon's Breath.[10]

– the author

BEHOLD: THE GOLDEN AGE

On August 17, 1987, the world celebrated the Harmonic Convergence. Had I known there was a connection between this event and my inner experience in Tibet, I would have planned my day differently. As it was, I celebrated the sacred event by watching two groups of adults trying to hit a little ball with a stick. I did learn the significance of that sunny day in August, however, a short while later. I learned that it had been a milestone in cosmic history.

There is an answer to every question a person has the wherewithal to ask. One should never be afraid to question—everything. The *energy of need* is just as substantial as the energy of electricity. It is this energy that is called into operation when we desire an answer to a question.

Who am I? Why am I here? Where am I going? These are but a few of the questions I had asked the universe in my nightly contemplations. The answers came from a variety of sources—books, dreams, friends, masters, myself. They didn't come all at once. In fact, my notebook of answers unfolded page by page over many years. One individual, however, has played an important role in my search for truth.

While hiking along the North Umpqua River in Oregon in my late teens, I met an elderly gentleman of partial Native American descent whom I'll call John Redstone. We met at *Colliding Rivers,* a viewpoint near the small community of Glide. Mr. Redstone was en route to Horse Heaven, a secluded valley located about seven miles up Horseheaven Creek, a tributary of Steamboat Creek, itself a tributary of the scenic North Umpqua. For seven days we backpacked together in the summer of 1970.[1]

As our friendship developed, I found Mr. Redstone to be an exceptionally kind and humble human being. He had learned a lot in his seventy-plus years upon the planet. Rather than calling himself a teacher, he preferred to say that he was simply sharing with others a few things that had helped him.

In the weeks following our first meeting, a powerful chieftain dressed in buckskins and a colorful headdress began appearing in my nightly dreams and contemplations. Although at the time I didn't make a conscious connection, while talking with friends I began referring to Mr. Redstone as "the Chief." It felt appropriate, so I continued. Within these pages the reference is meant as a gesture of respect.

This was the man who had afforded me the opportunity to witness the coming of the Dragon's Breath that magical night in Tibet, in August of 1987. Shortly thereafter, in a chance meeting at a farmer's market in southern Oregon, he reentered my life.

John Redstone greeted me warmly when I approached him in the parking lot behind the roadside tent. He recognized me immediately, even with my longer hair. The years had been kind to him. Now in his mid-eighties, he moved more deliberately, not in the spry, carefree way I had grown accustomed to on our trek up the Umpqua. But his eyes still sparkled with the same love of life as before.

I'd thought of him often since we'd said goodbye on a grassy knoll overlooking Horseheaven Creek so long ago. A small collection of parables and stories, pearls gleaned from our campfire chats, still occupied a dresser drawer that served as a file cabinet... and I still cherished the dream catcher, the gift he'd slipped into my pack without my knowledge. Finally I could thank him.

At our earlier meeting I'd been preparing for college. After initial pleasantries, he asked how my business training had worked out, politely overlooking the obvious answer. My shaggy hair and faded flannel shirt said it all. When I told him about my growing interest in spiritual subjects, specifically the changes taking place on the planet, he invited me to join him at his cabin for Sunday dinner. Thus began a series of conversations that would last, off and on, the better part of three years.

In the fall of 1987 John Redstone was living in a rented cabin on seven acres of land overlooking Little River near Colliding Rivers, a famous viewpoint on the way to Crater Lake in Oregon. Generally I would drive out to his cabin on Sunday evenings. Quite often our question and answer sessions lasted well into the night. To make this manuscript more readable, I have condensed these conversations and fictionalized peripheral details where I deemed appropriate. While at times I have chosen to convey the essence of the Chief's wisdom rather than his exact words, I have done my best to maintain the integrity of his ideas.

Little River meandered through the quiet meadow below us. Five hundred yards to the west it collided violently with the powerful North Umpqua, creating a breathtaking spectacle. The Chief poured two steaming cups of licorice root tea, then joined me on the back porch overlooking the river. It was good to rekindle our friendship and enjoy the sunset. That crisp September evening I learned the importance of the Harmonic Convergence and its relationship to the Dragon's Breath.

I began our conversation by asking the Chief (JR) about the Age of Aquarius, the "New Age;" specifically, how it would differ from the old one, the Piscean Age.

JR: "That's a good question, Michael, one that metaphysical schools across the board have been struggling to answer. Before we get into that, it might be helpful to take a quick look at cycles.

"As Earth travels on its journey around the sun, its magnetic pole points in turn to each of the twelve houses of the zodiac. The duration spent in each house is approximately 2,160 years. A great cycle on Earth's evolutionary spiral, the time it takes the planet to experience all twelve houses, lasts about 26,000 years. This is also the time it takes for our solar system to complete its orbit around the Alcyone (pronounced Al-SEE-ah-nee) spiral.[2] Alcyone is our Central Sun, the brightest star in the constellation Pleiades.[3]

"Now, these cycles don't begin and end abruptly. The strength of the outgoing cycle gradually diminishes while its successor gradually fades in. The resulting overlap zone depends upon the length of the cycle in question. Larger cycles require larger overlap zones.

"August 17, 1987, the Harmonic Convergence, was the midpoint of the 50-year Overlap Zone between the Piscean Age and the Age of Aquarius! If we count backwards from 1987 twenty-five years, we come to 1962. This is when the stronger energy of the Aquarian Age first made its presence felt upon the planet. Since that time it has gradually been gaining strength.

"Counting forward from 1987 twenty-five years we come to 2012, the date made famous by the Mayans. At this point, the lesser energy of the Piscean Age will reach its end-point. The Harmonic Convergence marked the time when the incoming energy of the Age of Aquarius and outgoing energy of the Piscean Age were equally balanced (Fig. 1). From that day forward, the Aquarian energy has been the more dominant of the two.

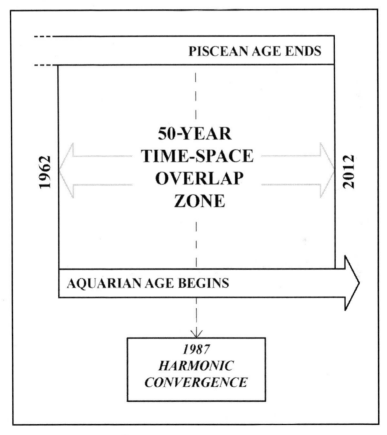

FIGURE 1: 50-YEAR OVERLAP ZONE

"Earth's entrance into a new age has always been a time of celebration and great change, but this will be one for the record books. There are several reasons for this. First of all, several major cycles are coming to a close. In addition to the two we just discussed (the 2,160-Piscean Age and the 26,000-year cycle), an even longer one discovered by the Mayan timekeepers is reportedly ending. It is a 104,000-year cycle made up of four 26,000-year cycles. When one of these grand cycles closes and a new one begins, humanity takes a well-deserved evolutionary leap. That leap is even more staggering when a solar system completes its epic journey around the galaxy at the same time. Our sun will accomplish this feat in 2012."

The Chief paused to take a sip of tea. It gave me a chance to ask him about the Dragon's Breath. Although he was surprised by my question—it was not a subject known to many—he went on to answer in detail without quizzing me about it. Later I told him about my inner experience with him in Tibet. He answered indirectly, neither confirming nor denying his part in it.

JR: "Ah, yes. This planet of ours is entering a spectacular band of multi-dimensional light known as the 'Photon Belt.' We first touched the edge during the Harmonic Convergence. In esoteric circles it is sometimes called the Dragon's Breath (Fig. 2). St. Germain called it the 'Golden Nebula,' a parallel universe of much higher vibration.[4]

"It emanates from the galactic center, where all archetypal ideas accessed by our sun and all suns in our galaxy originate. Twice every 26,000 years, when Earth enters Leo and later Aquarius, we re-visit this magnificent band of light. This historic passage happens like clockwork, without exception.

"Information about the Photon Belt is not new, it has just been suppressed. The closer we get to 2012, the more we will be hearing about this event. We must use discrimination, however, because much of the information will be false. [Chapter 10 contains additional information on 2012 and the Photon Belt from a number of independent sources.]

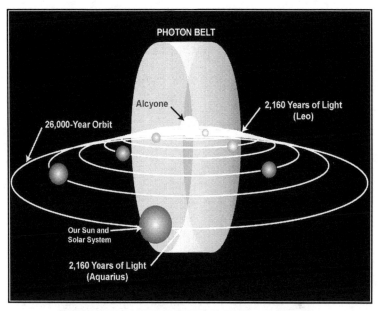

FIGURE 2: THE DRAGON'S BREATH

"There are those who know about the changes ahead, and are preparing for the physical disruption it will bring at this very moment. Unfortunately, those who hold power mistakenly believe that keeping the masses in the dark will be to their advantage somehow. Sadly, their actions will ultimately harm themselves."

M: "Will the new age officially begin on August 17th of 2012, or on December 21st as the Mayans predicted 5,000 years ago?"[5]

JR: "No one knows the exact date. Realistically it could occur within a two-year window on either side of 2012. The Gregorian calendar we use today was implemented under Pope Gregory in 1572. This was done intentionally to take us out of sync with the rest of the universe. Nature is tuned to 'Moon Time,' twenty-eight days and the thirteen cycles of the moon.[6] Life flows more harmoniously on 'Natural Time.' Furthermore, our present calendar, the one we deem so reliable and permanent, has been changed more than once in the past five hundred years.[7] This is why I give it two years either way."

M: "What is the purpose of the Dragon's Breath?"

JR: "It functions on many levels serving a variety of purposes, most of which are beyond our current understanding. We do know, however, that it acts as a transformer of cosmic energies, an initiator of sorts. It also revitalizes and heals all heavenly bodies that pass through its domain.

"At night when you and I go to sleep our bodies realign with the healing and balancing currents of the universe. In much the same way, the heavenly bodies need their time of rest. When the strain of daily life weighs heavily on our body, mind, and spirit, a warm shower can be very comforting. It also has a cleansing effect. Each time the Earth enters the Photon Belt, the planet experiences a much needed cleansing and rebalancing—its warm, soothing shower. After all, Earth is alive, too. The result is a Golden Age.

"You asked how the New Age would be different? A Golden Age is a period of abundance, happiness, peace, harmony, and longevity. Think of the happiest day of your life. This will give you some idea of what life will be like in the next cycle for those who have made the decision to better their lives. Even now, the higher Aquarian energy is assisting in the transition.

"We carry memories of past Golden Ages in our collective unconscious. Secretly we long for past times of joy and lightness, when life flowed effortlessly without struggle. Deep down we know that places like Shangri-la exist, for we have all lived during utopian times.

"Scholars summarily dismiss stories of men living to several hundred years of age as allegorical. But scholars generally have no knowledge of these golden cycles of the universe. With all the geological changes the planet has undergone in the past 12,000 years, few records remain to tell of past glories. Great libraries such as Alexandria have been burned to conceal the truth.[8] There are those who have the ability to access the Akashic records, however. The verification is there."

A large pot of beans had been simmering on the stove, enticing us through the open kitchen door. When the Chief invited me to join him for dinner, I readily accepted. The kitchen was tiny, but clean and uncluttered. A water purification device flanked the stainless steel sink along with a juicer and a combination steamer/rice cooker. Green and gold leaves decorated the white linoleum floor in both the kitchen and a well-stocked pantry. After setting the table, I waited in the living room for the dinner bell.

There was no television in the room, only a radio sequestered among several rows of books in an oak case that nearly matched the worn hardwood floor. Two matching beige recliners faced a large river-rock fireplace. A multi-colored throw rug near the hearth belonged to Goldie, the Chief's twelve year-old Golden Retriever. When I'd passed through on my way to the porch, I'd noticed several photographs on the mantle and a colorful painting centered above a blue, over-stuffed sofa.

The picture turned out to be a masterful reproduction of Van Gogh's *"Starry Night."* I found out later that the Chief had painted it himself. Three of the photographs dated back to the '30's or '40's. The same petite, dark-haired woman was in all of them. The four remaining photos featured waterfalls strung out along the North Umpqua Highway. A wallet-sized picture taped to the glass face of one of them caught my attention. Two men, one the Chief in his youth, sat in lotus fashion at the foot of a large tree. The other man wore a white turban, and appeared to be in his mid seventies.

When the Chief came into the room he found me gazing at the picture. The man in the photograph, he explained, was an East Indian guru known as the "Great Master." After a cup of beans, bread, and a salad in the living room, we continued our discussion of the coming changes.

JR: "This is a remarkable time to be alive. The coming of the Dragon's Breath is an historic event, but it will be eclipsed by an even more remarkable occurrence. Earth is graduating from the third dimension!

"Very soon we will be able to learn more in a year than we could in many lifetimes. How is this possible? Well, life is speeding up. You hear this on every corner. Fourth-dimensional energy is being released in greater and ever greater amounts from every cell in our body. This complements the increasing energy coming from the planet, itself.

"Planets evolve just as we do. In the schoolhouse of the universe, Earth is quite young and inexperienced. Most of the other planets in our galaxy have long since moved into higher dimensions on their evolutionary spiral."

M: "How will Earth's transition affect us?"

JR: "We will either raise our frequency with the planet or be held back. Those who need further experience in a dark and negative environment will have to look elsewhere for a home. Earth will no longer be an option. It is leaving behind the darkness of its past, especially the vibration of fear. This is why it is so important for us to clean house, so to speak. We are rapidly running out of time in this cycle. It is the eleventh hour on the cosmic clock, and everything changes at midnight. Are you feeling a bit like Cinderella?" The Chief smiled broadly.

"Many sincere individuals harbor a strong desire to heal the Earth. What they don't realize is that the planet has its own way of revitalizing itself. Soon, the Dragon's Breath will arrive on the scene in all its splendor and will facilitate the healing. Don't get me wrong, there are many worthwhile causes, but none are more important at this moment than getting our own house in order. [See Chapters 5 & 6 on the *Seedbed* and the *Mirror of Life* for suggestions regarding this daunting task.]

"Earth's graduation to a greater reality will change every facet of our lives. First of all, we will be reunited with loved ones who have crossed over to the astral plane. This fact alone should inspire us to forge ahead.

"We will also be able to communicate telepathically. All the cards will be 'face up.' Imagine what it will be like to know the thoughts of others. This will eliminate all trickery and deceit. Of course others will know our thoughts, as well. As for those flying dreams that are really astral experiences, once the transition is complete and man becomes more ethereal and less dense, these will be everyday occurrences. In time we will be able to manifest material objects with our thoughts, as we did in past Golden Ages. Goodbye Protestant Work Ethic. Hello, Freedom!

"No longer will we be at the mercy of those who control the power grid and 'Big Oil.' Free energy will be available to everyone. Are you beginning to see why this transition is so terrifying to those in power?"

M: "Yes. The changes will be greater than I imagined. But who decides who goes on with the planet?"

JR: "The spiritual hierarchy. But this is done quite mathematically. Everything vibrates at a particular frequency—our physical, mental, and emotional bodies, even our thoughts. At any given moment a composite average can be calculated. This is sometimes called our *mean energy floating point,* floating because it fluctuates with our changing thoughts and emotions. Base emotions and thoughts like anger and selfishness tend to lower our floating point. Consuming animal flesh and other coarse foods will also lower our vibrations.

"On the other hand, unselfish thoughts and acts of kindness raise our energy floating point. Infusing our thoughts and actions with the divine vibration of love will greatly accelerate our progress."

M: "How do we know what to work on?"

JR: "Prior to each incarnation we meet with spiritual counselors on the inner planes. They help us decide how much of our karmic baggage we can handle each time around, and what spiritual lessons we need to learn. God has given us His greatest gift, the gift of choice. But as co-creators we must take responsibility for all we create. This is where we have fallen short in the past. This is why the resolution of every problem must begin with taking responsibility for its creation. Most of our current problems have originated in other lifetimes. Since we have no recollection of these times, we complain of bad luck.

"But back to your question: What should we work on next? *Whatever is currently giving us physical discomfort, mental anguish, or emotional pain.* This will be our next challenge.

"It is our Higher Self that brings it to our attention. Once we have taken responsibility for creating the imbalance and have learned from the experience, then another unresolved issue can take its place."

M: "The world seems totally chaotic at this time. Do you think it can all be straightened out by 2012?"

JR: "Even though the world appears out of control, the universe is in perfect balance. Order is the first law of heaven, and balance is orchestrated in the worlds of time and space through the Law of Cause and Effect.

"You've seen how many people wait until the last minute to do their Christmas shopping? Well, there is a similar rush to take care of unfinished business here on Earth before the end of the current age. This is one reason why the planet is bursting at the seams. Everyone wants to be present for the finale, but it is 'invitation only.' Earth will go forward, either with or without us. Fortunately, the incoming energy of the Dragon's Breath is giving us a boost. But this also means that extra energy is available for those who have selfish motives.

"Twenty-twelve is not a magic line of demarcation. There may be limited pockets of resistance for a period of time thereafter—up to 50 years—as those who deal in negativity live out their lives.[9] When these people eventually pass over, however, the quality of life on Earth will improve dramatically.

"When it's time to be reborn, these destructive individuals will be asked to take their problems and lessons to a new world now being prepared for them by the hierarchy. They will have to contend with primitive and harsh conditions without the benefit of modern technology. Once again they will have to fight their way through jungles and search out caves for shelter."

I had several more questions, but it was getting late and I had to get up early the next morning for work. I ended our session with one last question.

"What will happen to the Earth after its 2,160-year cycle of the Photon Belt?"

JR: "It will progress into a higher frequency yet, a realm of intense light. For those individuals that go with it, communication by telepathy will be replaced with *knowingness*. There are some on this planet who are already working from this lofty level, or even beyond in the realms of *Pure Being*. But to answer your question, after passing through the Photon Belt, the fifth dimension will be the next stop on the journey of the *White Fire Beings*."

*   *   *

Man is in the process of changing
to forms that are not of this world;
grows he in time to the formless,
a plane on the cycle above. Know ye,
ye must become formless
before ye are one with the light.

– Adapted from *The Emerald
Tablets of Thoth*[10]

JOURNEY OF THE WHITE FIRE BEINGS

The Chief had painted a clear picture of where we are going, at least in the short run. Still I pondered my ultimate destination. In our next Sunday night session I learned the answer to this question, as well as answers to two other important ones: Who am I? Why am I here?

I found John Redstone, the man I affectionately called "the Chief," leaning against the porch railing when I arrived just after eight. He was throwing apples onto the lawn below for his "pets." A few minutes later a doe and her two fawns stepped gingerly out of an adjacent fir grove for their evening treat. They glanced wistfully at the Chief's garden spot as they passed. A ten-foot wire fence secured it from a variety of uninvited nocturnal guests, but mainly deer and raccoons.

Goldie greeted me as she'd done before. Her thick tail fanned wildly against my legs as she danced around and around in a circle licking at my hands. She then escorted me to one of the two sturdy wooden rockers where I awaited my friend's return from the kitchen with our tea. At his command, Goldie reluctantly retreated to her customary position in the corner of the small porch and sat down with a loud thud.

As our last discussion had ended, the Chief had made reference to "White Fire Beings." I had waited all week to ask him about them. As it turned out, this was one of his favorite subjects.

JR: "The White Fire Beings are God's great adventurers. They are Its pioneers and explorers. They function as God's eyes in worlds outside of Its own. But their home is the *Unchanging Ocean of Ecstasy,* the highest realm of Infinite Light. They are drops from the Ocean Itself. In a hundred million galaxies they wield the omnipotence of God. In a hundred million galaxies they do as they will. But here on Earth they are nearly powerless, for they have forgotten who they are. You see, *we* are the White Fire Beings!

"The story I am about to tell you may be a bit allegorical, but its origins are rooted in truth." The Chief closed his eyes and drew in a deep breath, savoring the opportunity to share a subject close to his heart. He was also careful to point out that the following story was his own interpretation.

"At a point independent of beginnings and endings, God roused Itself from sleep in the Unchanging Ocean of Ecstasy, Its eternal home. The first spark of consciousness sprang from a stirring of desire, a quality lying dormant in Its universal body. The primal moment of awakening manifested as *the desire To Be.*

"God found that It occupied all of Its world. It called Itself, '*I AM All That Is.*' There was no space/time continuum, there was no light or dark, no male or female, neither was there good or evil. There was no thought, nor was there emotion, for these are born of duality alone. There was only Oneness...and God was the only One.

"God went back to sleep. But this time It didn't lapse into unconsciousness. This time God dreamed. God dreamt of possibilities. Its dreams were magnificent, Its possibilities infinite. But they were only dreams. To manifest these possibilities required something God could not afford—another being.

"Being infinite has its problems. For one, how can an infinite being taste a huckleberry pie, one of God's many possibilities? This required being separate from the idea of the pie. It required individuality. Individuality was something God had plenty of, but it was 'infinite individuality.' It also required motion, but motion was born of duality.

"Eons passed as God contemplated Its problem. Finally It came up with a solution. To realize Its dreams and to experience their sweeping possibilities, It would have to implement a daring plan. God would have to venture forth from Its home in the Ocean of Light. It would have to descend into the abyss outside of Its universal body of Light and Sound, the realm of *All That Is Not!*

"While contemplating Its dilemma, God had looked within Itself and had discovered that It was composed of spirit sparks. How many? How many drops are there in the sea?

"God had figured out how to create a reality of duality and motion, but It needed help from the individual spirit sparks to do so. Some of these spirit sparks would have to isolate themselves from Divine Unity and embark on a perilous journey. Their charge? To experience *God's Great Dream of Possibilities* in the realm of All That Is Not.

"At first only a few brave spirit sparks volunteered to participate in the great experiment. The rest looked on with trepidation as their peers prepared to depart. These bold adventurers carried with them God's marvelous attributes, but also two powerful gifts God had given them to ensure success and safety on their great journey: the gift of imagination, and the gift of choice.

"As the spirit sparks left the Ocean of Light, God bestowed upon them a new name. It called them *White Fire Beings,* for they appeared as brilliant spheres of white-hot fire.

"These emissaries of God wielded Its ability to create, and soon myriad suns lit up the darkness of space. They created spinning planets of iridescent hues, and galaxies more numerous than the mind can conceive. Seven superuniverses surrounded God's wondrous abode.

"These daring pioneers who first signed on for the great experiment prepared those that followed for the coarse vibrations and violent emotions they would encounter in the lower worlds of time and space. Great schools were set up on the periphery of each sun in the numerous galaxies. They became the 'Seven Spheres of Cosmic Education,' one for each subject deemed necessary for survival. [These seven color bands of knowledge appear in the causal body of each individual that incarnates on a form world. No White Fire Being is allowed to embody on a form world without these seven bands that contain the total knowledge of all creation.]

"Some of the White Fire Beings were satisfied with the first sphere around the sun and stayed there. They exercised their gift of choice. Others stopped at the second or the third sphere, and found ways to serve God in these areas. A few of the more adventuresome ones completed their training and earned the right to experience life on physical worlds like our own.

"This journey produced two results. Through the White Fire Beings God was able to realize Its dreams. It was able to experience how it felt 'to be ocean,' for example, and how it felt 'to be in human form swimming in the ocean.' It was also able to experience how it felt 'to be accepted,' and how it felt 'to be shunned.' The spirit sparks benefited from the adventure, as well. Before their descent into the worlds of time and space, their only purpose had been self-amusement and play. In experiencing God's Great Dream of Possibilities, however, they developed spiritual maturity. Somewhere along the way they began giving to one another.

"For awhile the White Fire Beings experiencing life on Earth successfully tapped into the bands in their causal bodies. All knowledge in the universe was at their fingertips. But then something went wrong. Some of the beings living on other worlds misused their creative powers. They began to dominate other beings and refused to take responsibility for their actions. Their karmic debts grew massive. When their planets experienced a dimensional shift, these abusive beings were left behind to pay their debts to the universe.

"The spiritual hierarchy faced a dilemma. What could be done to assist these laggards? Well, somewhere between 300,000 and 400,000 years ago, the hierarchy made a fateful decision. They decided to send these wayward pioneers to Earth to finish their lessons.[1] It was believed that the good-hearted Souls on Earth would be a positive influence on them.

"But soon after these power-hungry individuals began reincarnating on Earth, they were back to their old tricks. With their vast experience at controlling others on their original planets, they found it easy to manipulate the innocent fourth root-race of man, even though their numbers were few. Misled, the original occupants of the planet lost their ability to think for themselves. They believed the lies fed to them in the contrived educational systems and confusing religious institutions founded by the transplants. They gave away their creative power. Worst of all, they lost contact with their seven bands of cosmic knowledge."

The Chief paused briefly, giving me an opportunity to break in with a question. "What has become of our color bands?"

JR: "We still carry them with us. This is why spiritual teachers have always proclaimed, 'the answers lie within.' But when man changed the nature of his thinking after the coming of the laggards, who set themselves up as the controlling elite, he lowered his vibrations to such a degree that he could no longer manifest his desires and needs. Words replaced pictures as the method of communication. He began controlling his emotions instead of feeling them. Whereas before he had been ethereal in nature, man became a dense, physical being.

"At this juncture in his evolution, man accumulated so much karmic baggage that it became impossible to take responsibility for it in a single lifetime; hence the origin of the 'Seedbed,' or Belief System. After splitting off a portion of the mind to act as a repository for this negativity, the spiritual hierarchy appointed the ego to oversee it. This was the actual 'fall of man,' not the fabricated story promoted by those seeking control." [The Seedbed is detailed in Chapter 5. It is the wall of ignorance that must come down before we can again access our color bands.]

M: "Will those who failed to graduate from their original planets progress with the Earth?"

JR: "Some will, but many have created further problems for themselves. Instead of bettering their lives, they have effectively dedicated their efforts toward holding as many people back from the transition as they can."

M: "Will we be aware of our color bands after 2012?"

JR: "This is the goal. Some, however, have already cleaned out their Seedbed and are presently enjoying full knowledge of who they are."

M: "Let me get this straight. Before each incarnation we agree to balance some of the unresolved issues in our Seedbed. We map out our life in advance. But if our experiences are planned ahead of time, where does free will fit in?"

JR: "Good question—predestination or free will? If I said both would it confuse you?" The Chief laughed good-naturedly, then went on to explain.

"When the White Fire Beings left the Unchanging Ocean of Ecstasy they were given the two gifts I mentioned earlier, the gift of imagination and the gift of choice. These can never be taken away—never. But when man changed the nature of his thinking and began to view himself as a physical body rather than a spiritual being, he forgot these powerful tools.

"Whether we are aware of it or not, we exercise the gift of choice every moment of our lives. Because of the dual nature of the creative power here on Earth, we can use it for manifesting either positive or negative ideas. The positive side of this energy is sometimes called *Prit*, and the negative, *Kal*.[2] They split off from the pure spiritual current flowing out of the Foun-

35

tainhead of God.[3] We choose what to think and our thoughts become reality. But when we allow others to mold our thinking, we create the version of reality *they* have chosen for us. This is exactly how we've been controlled and manipulated for countless centuries!

"Each and every moment we create future circumstances for ourselves. We choose. This is free will. But the Law of Self-Responsibility makes us accountable for our thoughts and subsequent actions. When we began creating more karma than we could balance in a single lifetime, it became necessary to store it in the Seedbed until later.

"So as not to overburden individuals returning to Earth with too much all at once, the spiritual hierarchy intervened. Counselors were appointed to meet with each individual prior to his incarnation. Together they plan out the life ahead, selecting specific events to accomplish the goal—the gradual reduction of the Seedbed without overwhelming, or even killing, the individual. These events, while allowing for free will, can be considered our destiny. Other factors shape our life experience, as well.

"If we set a mouse at the entrance to a maze, for example, it would have the choice as to which way to proceed; but the experience of 'the maze' (its destiny) has already been established for it. Furthermore, major choices are made prior to our incarnation—the time and place of our birth, for example, and our parents. All "milepost experiences" are pre-planned.[4] A story from Persia illustrates this point.

"In that ancient country there once lived a wealthy prince. Over the course of his life he had fulfilled every wish. Now, as he approached his twilight years, he had but one more dream to realize. He wanted to cheat the Angel of Death.

"The prince had heard of a famous magician who could manipulate the fabric of time and space. He had been known to disappear, and then reappear again in another place. One day the prince met with this powerful magician, and asked for his help. He asked the magician to transport him to India when the hour of his departure from this world drew nigh. Although the request was unusual, the magician volunteered his services—for a price. This feat would require much skill, he said, therefore the fee would be high. The prince agreed.

"When the time of the prince's passing was at hand, the magician flew into action. He used all of his powers. Amid a cloud of smoke and a flash of light, the prince disappeared; then, to his great astonishment and delight, he reappeared on the bank of the Ganges in India. But the prince's elation didn't last long.

"A shadowy figure approached carrying a thick, black notebook. It was the Angel of Death. Once the stunned prince had regained his composure, he asked the dark messenger how he had tracked him from Persia.

"'Persia?' the Angel of Death responded, glancing anxiously at his notebook. 'No,' he finally said, somewhat relieved. 'It says right here that I am to pick you up in India!'"

I smiled approvingly, wondering if my Higher Self had chosen the date of my own departure from this world.

M: "Are White Fire Beings our Higher Selves?"

JR: "You might call them that."

M: "Where is my Higher Self, somewhere inside my physical body?"

JR: "Although White Fire Beings, or Higher Selves, do invest a small portion of themselves within the bodies they manifest, their home is actually in the higher realms. The 'embodied fragment of White Fire' is called by different names: '*Soul,*' the '*I AM Presence,*' sometimes the '*Atma.*' Its headquarters is the permanent atom in the fifth chamber of the heart (on the supra-physical level).

"If we could magnify the I AM Presence millions of times, we would see the most beautiful, youthful likeness of ourselves encased in a translucent sphere of light, a three-fold flame of love, wisdom, and power cradling our divine aspect. Life-force originating in our Higher Self is drawn down through the silver cord, from which it then radiates.

"This fragment of White Fire also generates a powerful magnetic field that surrounds and interpenetrates the various bodies of man. This magnetic field is the recorder of every thought, feeling, or action that we have ever experienced [or ever will experience] as emissaries of the Divine."

M: "As we learn and grow, will we come to know our Higher Self?"

JR: "We don't actually have to *learn* anything. It's more of an 'unlearning and emptying-out' process. We strip away our limitations, we discard 'who we are not,' and in the end remember who we've always been. We awaken.

"In our present condition here on Earth, we feel isolated from our Divine Self. But separation is only in appearance. It is simply an illusion created by the mind. Ultimately we find that Soul, or the I Am Presence, is but an extension of our Higher Self. As a stream joins a river, so these two aspects of ourselves merge."

M: "And then the Higher Self returns to God, the Ocean?"

JR: "Yes. But first it must unite with itself, so to speak. It's not so much that the Self has been split, it is more of a temporary polarization. This had to be done in order to create within itself. After manifesting a portion of God's Great Dream of Possibilities in the worlds of time and space, however, these twin polarities unite."

[After our next discussion on the *light wave of creation* in Chapter 4, I had a better grasp of the masculine and feminine principles, also called positive and negative polarities, and the interchange between the two. In later discussions the Chief reemphasized that our return to Unity is actually one of realization, independent of time and distance. Since the mind cannot grasp formlessness or timelessness, it tends to interpret this awakening as a real journey, from point A to point B. For the time being, however, the Chief continued to speak in metaphors.]

M: "Does the Higher Self decide when this journey home to God begins?"

JR: "I'm sure that it does, or at the very least has some say in the matter." John Redstone's eyes narrowed. "I have often wondered, Michael, if, at the very moment we set out on this marvelous journey, the exact time and place of our eventual return was not also sealed. If this turns out to be the case, I'm certain that when this ancient appointment arrives we will know it in every fiber of our being. We will know that it is time for us to return home to the Unchanging Ocean of Ecstasy. When we do, our incredible journey as White Fire Beings will be over!"

The Chief smiled wryly. "But who knows what other adventures lie in store?"

*　　　　　*　　　　　*

We shall not cease from exploration,
and the end of all our exploring
will be to arrive where we started
and know the place for the first time.

　　　　　　　　　– T. S. Elliot[5]

SECRETS OF CREATION

On the drive out to Colliding Rivers my mind drifted back to a popular book I'd read in the early '70's, *The Third Eye*, by Lobsang Rampa, a famous Tibetan lama. A phrase from another of his books about life in Tibetan lamaseries intrigued me, "This is the world of illusion."[1] After some casual conversation about the new run of fall Chinook in the North Umpqua, I asked the Chief if he would explain the mysterious reference to our reality.

JR: "A good subject for this evening: 'Maya, the Queen of Illusion.' I wanted to touch on imagination in our last discussion. This topic will allow us to do so. Let's start with that.

"There is nothing in our imagination that does not exist in God's Idea of Creation, Its Dream of Possibilities. There is also nothing in our imagination that cannot be experienced 'somewhere' by exercising our gift of choice. This is the primary purpose of imagination—selection. We select from God's Great Dream of Possibilities.

"Now, God's Dream is complete in every detail. Creation is finished. It exists in the realm of All That Is. What we experience in our day-to-day life is not creation. *It is a reflection of creation, an illusion!* Consider the three-dimensional table upon which you ate breakfast this morning. Is it real?"

M: "I would say 'yes.'"

JR: "And how about a two-dimensional table projected upon the flat surface of a movie screen?"

M: "No."

JR: "Why do you say that?"

M: "When I'm seated in the theater, I can see the light from the projector in the back of the room. The table is just an image printed on film."

JR: "Let me ask you this. How would the table in the movie look to a two-dimensional character, also in the movie?"

M: "Hmm. I guess it would be real to him."

JR: "Of course. So what if your morning's breakfast was only a scene in a three-dimensional movie?" He paused momentarily for added effect. "If we could view the scene from a seat in a fourth-dimensional theater, would the table appear real?"

M: "Let's see... it would be real to the character, especially if his five senses were also part of the script. But from the viewer's perspective, it would not appear real."

JR: "That's right. Each time we rise above a plane we discover its illusory nature. We wake up."

M: "So where is the *actual* table?"

JR: "Reality exists in one place, and one place only —in the stillness of God's light in the realm of All That Is. Everything else is illusion. Everything else is a reflection.

"Hazrat Khan, the Sufi, echoed that life here is illusory when he said, 'If one could only know where the truth lies, what the truth is, if one could only know it and see it, one would understand that in reality all else is non-existent.'[2]

"This brings us to the dual nature of the universe. Three-dimensional objects are created by adding a second projector, a second light. To understand the interaction between these opposing lights is to understand the design of the atom, as well as the solar system. Both are variations of the same thing—a *light wave*."

The Chief asked if I was familiar with the Yin/ Yang symbol from the East (Fig. 3).

FIGURE 3: YIN/YANG SYMBOL

I borrowed his words for my answer. "Isn't it supposed to depict the dual nature of the universe?"

JR: "Yes, it does. The light flows into the darkness, and in return, the darkness flows into the light. They become each other."

M: "What are the two dots, the white dot in the middle of the dark circle, and the black dot inside the white one?"

JR: "The white dots are suns, and the black dots are black holes. Suns and black holes could be considered opposite ends of the same stick, the stick being the polarity shaft of a light wave. Both are reflections of the One Light extended from the fulcrum point in the center of the wave. This brings the total to three, the number of creation." The Chief smiled at my puzzled expression.

"I'll explain further about the light wave in a minute, but let's back up for a moment. What do we know? We know that creation is finished, right? Creation exists as God's Great Dream of Possibilities in the still light of Unity. We know that creation exists in the form of a hologram; that is, we know it isn't possible to take a single idea and separate it from the whole. But it *is* possible to select an idea by using the imagination and take a picture of it, so to speak. The image will appear backwards because it is a reflection of the original idea.

"This picture can then be split into opposites within a light wave. This is the true purpose of mind—to create duality. For this reason, we cannot experience Divine Unity by thinking about it. By using our imagination, we can select anything we want to experience from God's Palette of Still Ideas. Our thinking then sets the idea into motion in a light wave. It is expressed, then voided back to stillness when its purpose is fulfilled. We see only the active, or expressive, phase. We cannot see the voidance half of the cycle, the reaction. It vibrates beyond the range of our senses.

"As in our present-day movies, each picture in the expressive phase is slightly advanced from the one in the previous frame. The gap in-between each frame is similar to the voidance phase. When still pictures are flashed across the projector light, an illusion of motion is created. Similarly, the events in our lives are projections on a bigger screen.

"In *Autobiography of a Yogi*, Paramahansa Yogananda observed that 'one's values are profoundly changed when he is finally convinced that creation is only a vast motion picture; and that not in it, but beyond it, lies his own reality.'[3]

"In 1915 Yogananda witnessed a strange vision that helped him understand the eternal light of Unity behind the painful dualities of Maya. It happened during the time the First World War was raging across Europe. Suddenly, his consciousness was transferred to the body of a captain in command of a battleship. A huge shell hit the powder magazine and tore the ship asunder. Surviving the explosion, the captain jumped into the water, only to be struck in the chest by a stray bullet. As the mysterious footsteps of death caught up with the captain, Yogananda found himself once again in his tiny room on Garpar Road.

"A dazzling play of light filled the whole horizon, Yogananda explained, and a soft rumbling vibration formed itself into words: 'What has life or death to do with light? In the image of My light I have made you. The relativities of life and death belong to the cosmic dream. Behold your dreamless being! Awake, My child, awake!'[4]

"Shortly thereafter, Yogananda described a similar vision in which he experienced the motion picture of his body in the faintly lit theater of his bedroom. A voice spoke as if from the light above him: 'This is the cosmic motion-picture mechanism. Shedding its beam on the white screen of your bed sheets, it is producing the picture of your body. Behold, your form is nothing but light!'"[5]

M: "Do suns and black holes play a part in the cosmic motion picture?"

JR: "What's the best way to answer that?" The Chief furrowed his brow, gazing off into space. "There is but one substance in all the universe—light! But there are many conditions of light, pressure being one. Light, when compressed, can be heated to white-hot incandescence, hence the sun. This is sometimes called the *father-light*. When the self-same light is expanded and cooled, it becomes the dark *mother-light* of space. The father-light holds a positive charge, but the mother-light has no charge. It is sometimes called 'negative.' Energy flows from the highest electrical potential to the lowest; hence the interchange between the sun and space.

"Walter Russell spoke of this interchange in his book, *The Secret of Light*. He noted that all suns are generated into incandescence by two black rivers of evacuated light that flow inward toward their still centers by way of the poles. Conversely, the darkness of space is radiated from two incandescent rivers of white light that flow centrifugally from suns' equators (Fig. 4).[6]

"As in the Yin/Yang symbol, the dark mother-light of space *becomes* the incandescent father-light of the sun and vice versa. Opposites are born from each other. The black hole in the center of a sun is the first stage of this transition in a solar system. Astronomers report these occurrences as 'ringed nebula.'

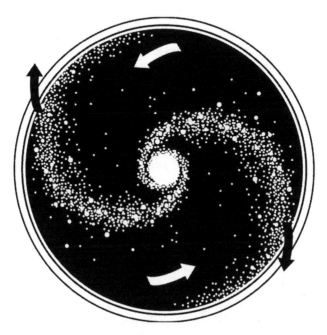

FIGURE 4: THE FOUR RIVERS OF LIGHT[7]

"This demonstrates the Law of Giving, or the Law of Love. One half of the cycle gives its energy to its opposite, which in turn, re-gives its energy to the other. This is called *Rhythmic Balanced Interchange*. In practical terms, each action becomes its own reaction. The universe is self-balancing!

"The two opposing lights projected through each other provide the variety of conditions necessary for the manifestation of physical reality, whether they be electrons in an atom, minerals in the Earth, tissues in a body, or planets in a solar system. The various elements in the periodic table are not different things.

They are only different pressure conditions of the one substance, light.

"All light waves are cube-shaped vacuum chambers similar to the picture tube in your television set. The dark mother-light of space is defined by six mirrored sides comprised of inert gasses at zero points of motion. This prevents the idea being expressed in one light wave from interfering with an idea being expressed in a neighboring one.

"When ideas are expressed, they are radiated out from the sun toward the blackness of space. When they are voided, they flow back from the cold cube toward the incandescent sphere. Radiation is the negative, centrifugal force; gravity is the positive, centripetal one. The cube and the sphere are the father and mother of all other forms. Every object is either becoming a cube, or becoming a sphere. From our earthly perspective, ideas are frozen into form, then voided through melting by extreme temperatures.[8] The expressive phase is sometimes called the *Outbreath of God,* the voidance phase, the *Inbreath.*

"The polarity shaft of the light wave runs north and south. Ideas are always expressed in a northerly direction. This is why time runs in only one direction from our perspective—north.

"Light doesn't travel at 186,400 miles per second as science claims. In fact, being a quality of God, light doesn't travel at all. What we call the speed of light is actually the velocity at which the light wave turns inside out after each half-cycle to maintain a northerly direction in a spiral pattern. The idea is reflected from wave field to wave field in this manner. This accounts for the 'flow of time.'

"Ideas are actually expressed and voided simultaneously. There is no interval of time between the two, for both are opposite mirror images of one another, extended from a common center. Since the reaction half of the cycle vibrates beyond the range of our senses, the illusion of continuity and time is perpetuated. If it did not, there would be no 'cosmic movie.'"

It was difficult for me to grasp this illusion of motion. I did have one frame of reference, however. While in grade school I'd been given a deck of cards. On the first card was the picture of a horse. The rest of the deck featured the same horse, but in each successive card its legs were in slightly advanced positions. As I fanned the cards, the horse appeared to be running. The Chief continued.

"In the center of the polarity shaft is a still point of mind, the *fulcrum,* where the energy exchange between opposites takes place. It is also the point where our two-way electric universe of thinking extends at a 90-degree angle from the still magnetic universe of knowing. All power, all knowledge, all love, all light, and all consciousness originate in stillness. This zero point of motion also serves as the communication center for the light wave.

"We've talked about how each idea is expressed in a vacuum so as not to interfere with its neighbors. We wouldn't want a pine tree to sprout a furry tail instead of a bough, for example, would we? I suppose then we would have to call it a 'fur' tree!" The Chief laughed for several seconds at his joke.

"Even though each light wave appears isolated from the rest, God has devised a vast communication network to coordinate all activities in Its myriad universes. It is known as the 'Golden Thread.' Some call it the 'Golden River,' because, when viewed from the spiritual planes, it shimmers like a golden river of light dancing upon the sea.

"Light waves are connected to each other at the fulcrum point by the Golden Thread. No matter how insignificant the action within a particular light wave, the effect ripples across the fabric of time and into eternity, touching everything in existence. There truly are no secrets in the universe due to the energy of the Golden Thread.[9] This is how God extends Its omnipresence, even unto the dream worlds of Maya, the realm of All That Is Not."

M: "Is there a consciousness associated with the Golden Thread?"

JR: "Yes, there is... 'Total Consciousness.'"

The Chief's answer caught me by surprise and touched a nerve. Have you ever suddenly remembered that you'd forgotten something extremely important, but couldn't quite put your mental fingers on it? That was the sensation.

M: "What is meant by vibrations?"

JR: "The frequency at which the opposites within a light wave interchange at the fulcrum. To put it another way, the time it takes for Yin to become Yang, and vice versa. The Rhythmic Balanced Interchange is regulated by tone, or sound. This is why certain spiritual techniques involve the chanting or singing of a word to change the vibrations. Specific sounds and repetitions can increase or decrease the vibratory frequency of the various bodies of man. Everything in creation vibrates in accordance with its own unique keynote, which emanates from the fulcrum. Everything in the universe is continuously proclaiming its identity. It is singing 'I am an elm tree,' or 'I am a grain of sand'... 'I am Michael!'" The Chief flashed a quick smile.

"The grand symphony of the universe has been poetically called the *Music of the Spheres*. It is also known as the Audible Lifestream, or Sound Current. Each group of minerals, each family of plants, each species of animals, together with the human family, all add their keynotes to the chorus of this planet. Planets harmonize with galaxies, galaxies with universes. Even the individual planes of God can be identified by specific sounds.

"Beginning with the physical world, these sounds include thunder, the roar of the surf, the tinkling of bells, running water, and the buzzing of bees. In the realms of undivided light, these sounds become even more enchanting—the single note of a flute, a heavy wind, a deep electrical hum, a thousand violins, the music of woodwinds, the sound of a whirlpool, the music of the universe, and the music of God.[10]

"Mystics agree that in the highest heavens the sound finally becomes *HU*, the most sacred of all sounds.[11] According to Hazrat Khan, HU is the beginning and end of all sounds, be they from man, bird, beast, or thing. The Supreme Being has been called by various names in different languages, but the mystics have known Him as HU, the natural name, not man-made, the only name of the Nameless, which all nature constantly proclaims.[12] The Vairagi Masters sing HU and *Aluk* as mantras.[13] AUM, a sound symbol from the mental plane, can also be used to tune into the Inner Sound.[14]

"Some train themselves to hear the Music of the Spheres in the solitude on the sea shore, on the river bank, and in the hills and dales; others attain it while sitting in the caves of the mountains, or when wandering constantly through forests and deserts, keeping themselves in the wilderness apart from the haunts of men. Yogis and ascetics blow horns or shells, which awakens in them this inner tone. Dervishes play a double flute for the same purpose. The bells and gongs in churches and temples are meant to suggest to the thinker the same sacred sound, and thus lead them towards the inner life."[15]

M: "What are thoughts?" Whenever I attempted to sit still for any length of time, a parade of thoughts raced through my mind. They seemed to have a life all their own and behaved very badly during my contemplations.

JR: "Thinking is the process of extending idea into form by seemingly dividing it into opposites in a light wave. But of course an idea cannot be split from the whole; it is a reflection. We could say that thought forms are reflections of still ideas encased in vacuum chambers for the purpose of simulating motion. The quality and type of thought determines the vibratory frequency, and hence, the emotion generated. Both thought and E-motion (energy of desire in motion) create the complete experience. This is why we cheat ourselves, and the Divine experiencing Itself through us, when we suppress our emotions.

"With imagination, we choose which ideas we want to experience from God's Great Palette of Possibilities, sometimes called the 'Morphogenic Field of Ideation.' In the stillness of God's Indivisible Light, creation is finished. The palette is complete. A limited selection from this palette is made available to a form world, however, when it is ready for human habitation. During each subsequent evolutionary cycle, God adds to this limited palette from which we draw our ideas. As we speak, the *new fourth-dimensional codes* are being installed in our planet's morphogenic field. Out with the old ideas, in with the new.

"Once selected, ideas are then split into opposites within light waves in the solar plexus region, the abdominal brain, and are then set in motion. (Our brain is actually the receiver of thoughts.) At this point, they are called 'thought forms.' Before they are materialized, however, they take a short detour out to the Van Allen Belt, where they are reflected back to Earth after a built-in 24-hour delay.

"At any time during this period we can cancel any thoughts we don't want materialized. We can say something like: 'In the name of my I Am Presence, I call upon my Higher Self to cancel any harmful or unkind thoughts that I may have sent out in the last 24 hours.' I always picture myself erasing the unwanted thoughts from an imaginary chalkboard while repeating the words."

M: "How do thought forms know where to return? Do they ever come back to the wrong person?"

The Chief smiled broadly at the question. "No. They go out with our individual electronic keynote attached to them. It's like our cosmic signature.[16] Once these thought forms are cleared for manifestation, their vibrations are slowed down and they are compressed into matter. They must obey the Law of Rhythmic Balanced Interchange, just as any other light wave. Compression and expansion produce the same dual father/mother lights.

"The air we breathe and the water we drink furnish the raw materials needed for the expansion and compression process. Hydrogen compresses and solidifies a thought into matter; oxygen expands and liberates it. Specifically, it is the fire within the oxygen that does the work. Science calls this oxidation."

M: "How long can a thought stay in manifestation?"

JR: "Unless thoughts are held in consciousness, they are automatically voided." The Chief gazed out into the warm autumn night, searching for the appropriate words. Finally he ran his fingers through his hair and continued. "Every thought has a purpose for which it is created. When that purpose is fulfilled, it is returned to stillness. But during the life of the thought it must be continuously held in consciousness. This is the function of the elemental kingdom.

"*Elementals* are unique beings trained in the art of concentration. They're on the same evolutionary spiral as the angels. As the 'builders and holders of form,' they provide a valuable service to the hierarchy. We have these worker bees to thank for virtually everything we encounter from birth to the grave. Their portfolio of work includes everything from planets to petunias. Advanced elementals go through rigorous training. To hold a common oak tree in manifestation, for example, requires an army of lesser elementals. An experienced supervisor must coordinate their activities.

"When we hear about elementals, we generally think of 'Nature Spirits.' There are four groups in this category, each one associated with an element: air, earth, fire, and water. Sylphs are the delicate fairies of the air; gnomes, the little people of the forest; salamanders are the dragons of the fire; and undines, or water spirits, are the mermaids of the sea. The vibrations of the elemental kingdom are somewhat higher than those of mankind. However, a few people have had the ability to see beyond the normal range and have immortalized them in pictures.

"Each I AM Presence, or Soul, that embodies on a form world is assigned a 'body elemental' by the hierarchy. This advanced elemental builds the physical body during each incarnation according to the blueprints furnished by the I AM Presence. The elemental also maintains the body's numerous involuntary functions. To accomplish these tasks, the advanced elemental must recruit and supervise countless millions of lesser elementals. Together they serve the individual over the course of the entire lifestream.

"Between embodiments the I AM Presence and the body elemental separate. The I AM Presence goes into the astral realm for cleansing and rejuvenation; the elemental returns to its home sphere surrounding the sun for much needed R & R and encouragement. The year 2012 will be a welcome milestone in the life of many body elementals, as well, for their long tour of duty in the physical universe will be over."

It was nearing eleven p.m., and my eyes were getting heavy. But my growing curiosity about 2012 wouldn't let me rest.

M: "In the early 1970's Ruth Montgomery wrote a book called *A World Beyond*.[17] In it she talked about the shifting of the Earth's magnetic poles. Edgar Cayce also predicted a polar shift in the winter of 1997-1998.[18] Will this be a concern?"

JR: "I don't know the exact date, but I can tell you this: the Earth's poles will flip. This is because we are approaching the end of the Outbreath cycle for our solar system and galaxy.[19] When we begin the return, the Inbreath, Earth's magnetic poles must shift! The Law of Rhythmic Balanced Interchange will see to this." The Chief could see by my furrowed brow that more explanation was needed.

"The shift is really an electrical phenomenon. One polarity stores electrical potential until a certain point is reached. A reversal of the poles allows for the discharge of this electrical energy, which then flows in the opposite direction toward the lower electrical potential. Since our solar system is a light wave—and if the ancient calendars are accurate—then we can expect a magnetic shift somewhere around 2012."

M: "What is Zero Point?"

JR: "It is the fulcrum of the light wave, a zero point of both motion and energy. Think of a swinging pendulum. For the briefest moment, just as it reaches its maximum arc on either side, it must stop before changing directions. In like fashion, there is a pause at the end of each Outbreath [and Inbreath] of God. Time must stop. At this still point, creation reaches its potential. The idea has been expressed. It then re-gives its energy to its counterpart at the fulcrum, or Zero Point. This is when the polarity of the system will reverse.

"At that moment we will experience a peace beyond all understanding, for the forces that normally weigh us down will have been suspended momentarily. We must keep our composure, however, for the traditional electrical systems that stem from motion, including lights and phones, will temporarily cease to function. For the uninformed masses, this will be a time of great fear."

I remembered a Native American prophecy that said the sun will rise in both the east and west on the same day.[20] It prompted another question.

M: "Will the Earth spin in the opposite direction after the shift?"

JR: The Chief's eyes twinkled. "Would it be so bad to watch the sun *rise* over the Pacific for a change?" I took this as a "yes."

M: "What kind of damage can we expect?"

JR: "No one knows for certain at this point what Earth changes will accompany the magnetic shift. Structural damage isn't a given. However, regions needing purification by fire or water may be susceptible to volcanic eruptions or shifting landmasses. Personally, it doesn't matter to me whether I'm living here, or translate to the inner worlds.

"Something tells me the devastation won't be as great as many have predicted. The shift may be quite gentle. We shouldn't worry too much about the future, anyway, Michael. It will find us wherever we are." The Chief smiled reassuringly.

"Furthermore, the future isn't cast in stone. As mankind raises its collective consciousness, Earth changes will be lessened.[21] When one person makes the decision to better his life, the whole world prospers. This is why nothing is more important than getting our own house in order. We can only do this in the present moment."

*　　　　*　　　　*

Time is not at all what it seems;
it does not flow in only one direction,
and the future exists simultaneously
with the past.

– Albert Einstein[22]

PART II

A RETURN TO SELF-KNOWLEDGE

UNDERSTANDING THE SEEDBED

Few places in the world can rival Oregon's colorful, late-September wardrobe—its gold and red leaves, its blue-green rivers, its emerald forests of pine, fir, and spruce. On my next trip to see the Chief we opted for a walk rather than our customary gathering place on his porch. It was a breezy, sunny afternoon, just right for an invigorating hike along Little River. Goldie bounded ahead with puppy-like enthusiasm, stopping occasionally to test the wind for the scent of quail and pheasant.

After half an hour we doubled back along the paved road that led to the Colliding Rivers viewpoint. As much as I enjoyed the tranquility of Little River, the rugged cliffs and churning white rapids of the Umpqua fired my imagination. I always gravitated to Colliding Rivers at turning points in my life, perhaps to reconcile the different sides of my own nature.

Soon the rough-hewn bench came into sight where I'd met the Chief seventeen years earlier. Usually my mind chattered with a hundred questions, but this particular Sunday I had none. It was enough to enjoy the view, and to listen to the Chief talk about his gardening and canning pursuits. The small space relegated to his vegetables occupied approximately six hundred square feet, but it provided him with all he wanted... and there was always extra to share with neighbors.

While reflecting on the Chief's 'modest abundance,' a seminar I had once attended at a New-Thought church came to mind. It also sparked an important discussion about the Belief System. As I recounted my experience, I detected a glint of restrained humor dancing in the Chief's kind eyes.

I'd gone with several friends to hear the "Queen of Prosperity" at a local church. "You can have whatever you want!" she proclaimed with great conviction, pacing back and forth across the stage like a tigress defending her young. "You are a person of power!" Her presentation combined the fervor of a bible-thumping revival with the salesmanship of an infomercial.

After her main spiel, it became apparent how the Queen filled her coffers. She suggested with obvious transparency that each of us send money to the person who furnished our spiritual food. She passed the hat a bit too quickly for my taste.

JR: "Well, she was half-right." The Chief leaned back against the hard bench with a smile. "We *can* have whatever we want, but the second half of the statement is this: *as long as it is in harmony with our Belief System.* This is the one piece of information missing from practically every New Age philosophy. This missing piece is a source of doubt and great frustration for those doing everything possible to manifest their dreams.

"The Belief System has aptly been called the Valley of Pain and Disillusionment. It is the symbolic wasteland that stands between man and his next stop on this marvelous journey. Each person must cross this wasteland under his own power, but any number of teachers and masters are always nearby. They can provide valuable guidance if asked. Moreover, the fourth-dimensional energy now being released upon the planet by the Dragon's Breath is available for our use.

"To recap for a moment, the Belief System, or 'Karmic Seedbed,' came into being when mankind began creating more negativity than it could balance in a single lifetime. The hierarchy split off a portion of the mind to act as a repository for this information, placing the ego in charge. The fine vibrations of our Higher Self cannot come in contact with negativity; therefore, we must clean out the Seedbed before progressing into the higher planes. This is the emptying-out process that we talked about earlier.

"The Belief System also became a storehouse for all the misconceptions, crippling judgments, suppressed emotions, and negative thoughts that haunt our waking lives. Although we generally aren't conscious of our Belief System, its contents are out-pictured into physical reality on a day-to-day basis. This results in problems, accidents, fears, and addictions. When we lost touch with our seven color bands of cosmic knowledge, the Seedbed became our 'guidebook for living.'

"Our every wish, hope, dream, and prayer must be qualified by the Belief System unless couched in picture form. The ego scrutinizes every thought to insure that it conforms to the contents of the Seedbed. When there is a conflict between our thoughts and the Belief System, the Belief System always wins. [The

63

Chief was speaking of thoughts, here, not imagination.]

"For example, let's say we have adopted a deep-rooted belief from an orthodox upbringing that states: 'It is harder for a rich man to enter the Kingdom of Heaven than it is for a camel to go through the eye of a needle.' To reinforce this belief, we observe successful businessmen engaged in deceptive practices.

"Then one day we are presented with an opportunity to make a lot of money in a business deal. As our unseen advisor, the ego surveys the prospective deal and says to itself, 'Oh my, we could make a lot of money on this one. If we do, then we will be rich. If we're rich, then we won't go to heaven.'

"This is the way the Belief System operates—by association. Since we are going against the rules we have agreed to live by, the ego throws a monkey wrench in the works, so to speak. While its scope is limited, the ego does hold the power to shape physical events. It could manifest an unexpected auto expense, for example, or we might get an expensive speeding ticket and use up the money we had set aside for our investment. Even though we may have changed religions, we could still carry the 'rich man and the camel curse' as a judgment in our Seedbed."

M: "Is the ego conscious?"

JR: "It is actually very mechanical and computer-like in nature. But over the course of countless lifetimes an illusory being takes shape. The ego can appear to take on a personality of its own. The nature of this personality depends upon the judgments we hold: *I am rich; I am poor; I am unappreciated; I am appreciated*... the list goes on and on.

"If we've held positions of power or prestige in the past, we may have cultivated judgments of self-importance. Armed with enough of these assumptions from many past incarnations, the ego can become very proud of itself. It will rush to take credit for our spiritual progress if it finds beliefs of arrogance or self-importance in the Seedbed. The ego will say, 'Look at me, I am a great spiritual being.'" The Chief laughed. "From the higher perspective, of course, there is no *I;* there is only *All.*"

M: "Is there a way to stop the ego from sabotaging our plans?"

JR: "As strange as it may sound, in its own deviant way the ego is actually working for our benefit. It uses everything in its limited power, including fear and deception, to ensure that we stay safe and secure within the bounds of our comfort zone, the Seedbed. The ego can even take on the role of 'dream censor' in our nightly dreams.

"'Threshold guardians' of myth also fit the description of the ego. They show up in the guise of well-meaning friends and loved ones whenever we attempt to brave the unknown in our quest for self-knowledge. According to these threshold guardians, terrible things await us if we break with the confines of traditional thinking—in other words, the comfort and safety of our Belief System. The jungle is a dangerous place. Those foolish enough to venture far from the village of mediocrity end up the supper of lions and tigers.

"Stern warnings charged with guilt and fear come from the pulpit, as well. We must conform, be steadfast, endure, and follow the scriptures to the letter (no matter how many times they've been changed). Threshold guardians caution us against leaving the flock. We could burn for eternity, or lose our very Soul." The Chief shook his head.

"Karl Marx had the ego pegged when he uttered the famous words, 'The road to hell is paved with good intentions.'[1] The ego will sabotage our happiness without hesitation if it finds contrary patterns in our Seedbed. But it sleeps like a baby at night because its intentions are good. It has our best interest at heart.

"Its primary goal is our protection. You see, the ego knows that when we think and act out of context with our Belief System, it's like plugging a 220-volt appliance into a 110-volt outlet. When this happens, trouble follows. This 'short-circuiting' results in inefficient metabolism on the cellular level. New cells get altered, and a fine, electromagnetic acid-ash accumulates, blocking the flow of water and nutrients. **This is why all changes must be made at the level of the Belief System.**"

M: "How do we know what judgments and other garbage is stored in our Seedbed?"

JR: "We have no way of knowing, but knowing isn't necessary. As we talked about earlier, our Higher Self will bring to our attention the next thing we need to balance.

"The bulk of our Seedbed can be traced to prior lifetimes. Irrational fears, for example, stem from past traumas—being buried alive, falling over cliffs (or being pushed), drowning...the list goes on and on. While horrible deaths leave lasting impressions, any event infused with strong emotions can adversely affect our future. Since we have no recollection of the past, solutions are often elusive."

M: "Can you give me an example of this?"

JR: The Chief thought for a moment. "Sure. Many health-conscious people find it difficult to maintain weight or strength while following a vegetarian diet. They turn to health care professionals who convince them that some people 'just need meat in their diet.' Since they have no knowledge of the Belief System, this is a fair assumption. Often these authorities will argue strenuously against vegetarianism. This is a tip-off that contrary belief patterns lie buried in their Seedbed.

"We have all been hunters in numerous incarnations. Picture this: A young Indian brave is seated before a ceremonial campfire beneath a blanket of stars. The smell of roasting meat wafts on the breeze. Seated around the circle are tribal elders, each one a tested warrior. The boy's heart pounds with excitement in concert with rhythmic drums, anticipating his first buffalo hunt. 'Eat your meat,' the elders tell him. 'Meat will make you strong for the great hunt tomorrow!'

"A powerful scene like this can greatly affect an impressionable youth... and this is but a single scene from a single lifetime. Imagine hundreds or even thousands more, all adding to the complexity of the Belief System. Without our conscious knowledge, they become the rules we have agreed to live by until higher understandings take their place. But back to our meat example.

"One day at the urging of friends we agree to try a vegetarian diet, unaware of strong belief patterns lodged within our Seedbed. Soon after eliminating all animal protein, however, we begin to lose weight. Since our friends are doing fine, we conclude that the trouble lies within us.

"Unconsciously we seek out health care professionals who have similar judgments in their Belief Systems. With the light of ancient campfires dancing in their eyes they tell us matter-of-factly, 'Have a steak. Our bodies need meat to make us strong (for the great hunt tomorrow).'

"The desire for meat is an electromagnetic pull that leads directly to the Seedbed. When we cut out meat without first changing our belief patterns, we run into problems. Our bodies require meat to function properly. This is what the blueprints in our Seedbed call for, thus we crave it. However, once we upgrade the Belief System and our body is 'rewired,' our desire will cease. We won't have to deny ourselves meat. In fact, it will taste quite unappetizing.

"Many of our health problems stem from the past when we have indiscriminately taken life in both the animal and the human kingdom. The Law of Cause and Effect is timeless. Since we have spilled blood, the ingesting of blood through meat eating is likely connected."

I told the Chief that I had seen firsthand how judgments shape our lives. I'd worked with a man named Robert, a big meat-eater, at a plywood mill while in high school. Every day Robert arrived for work exactly one hour early. I never tired of asking him about this, and always received the same reply. "My old man used to tell me," he'd say with a broad grin and a goofy laugh, "it's better to show up for work one hour early than a minute late." I also related a personal example to the Chief.

"My father was a mining engineer in the Pacific Northwest." The Chief conveyed his interest with a nod. "I spent most of my childhood moving from mining camp to mining camp. As you might imagine, the houses we lived in were often on the verge of condemnation. I don't know how my mom put up with it.

"Hard times came all too often, but she had a special knack for looking on the bright side. When things got a little tight she would smile and say, 'Don't worry, we'll always have enough.'

"And true to her belief, we always *did* have enough. But as good as that sounds, we never had *more than enough!* It was quite a shock to realize how many ways her life had been affected, and how surely her belief had become my own."

The Chief nodded in agreement.

JR: "Judgments are harmful because they limit our future possibilities. When we make a judgment we are saying to ourselves, 'every future experience will be just like the one we had.' Even the tiniest of judgments can greatly limit our life experience. Let me give you an example.

"An acquaintance of mine was given an apple when he was nine years old. The apple was the softest, mushiest, most tasteless Red Delicious apple that you can imagine. My friend formed a judgment: "Apples taste bad." For over a decade, not an apple touched his lips. Then one day he was given a Gala apple. Reluctantly he tried it. It was wonderful! He began to enjoy other kinds of apples, even Red Delicious. He realized that the seemingly insignificant judgment he'd made at the age of nine had greatly affected his life.

"Furthermore, judgments produce a false view of reality. If I made the statement 'boats are dangerous,' would this be an accurate assessment of boats? No. Contrary to my personal bias, boats are generally pretty safe. More than likely the reality of the situation is this: I fell off a boat once, nearly drowned, and have not yet released the fear."

M: "How do we get rid of these judgments?"

JR: "Very simple. We transmute them through understanding. *A higher truth will always transmute a judgment of lower frequency.* This is done automatically by the ego, but it is helpful to verbalize our new understanding. The vibration of sound will also aid in releasing any trapped emotions surrounding the judgment. Using the example you just mentioned, we can say something like, 'I release the judgment that I'll always have enough; I accept the truth that I will always have an abundance.'

"One more thing, Michael. We must always put our thoughts into picture form. This is the first step in the Golden Formula, a template for upgrading the Belief System."

M: "Why pictures?" An old Pontiac pulled into the viewpoint and three teenagers piled out. Two of them strolled over to the rock wall near our bench and waited for their friend to return from the restroom. The Chief flashed them a warm smile as they retreated to their car. When they were out of earshot, he continued.

JR: "Pictures are the true language of the mind. They operate above the level of the Belief System. This is why positive thinking or repeating affirmations doesn't work. If good does come of it, it can only be temporary. Their vibrations aren't high enough to trump the strong belief patterns in the Seedbed. But imagination is.

"We have been taught that imagination is simply the whimsical meanderings of a child-like mind. This has been done intentionally to keep us trapped in dependence-mode. But even though we have lost conscious contact with our causal body, we can still tap into this reservoir of truth and gain our freedom by using the imagination.

"To establish self-knowledge we must first start with a familiar image. Other images will unfold like pages on a flip chart. When we hold our attention on a concept in this manner, our Higher Self looks at it from its lofty position. Remember, it is still in contact with the Universal Knowledge. While the information may not be available to us on a conscious level at this point, it will be stored in our subconscious mind to be accessed later. When we need the information, it will be there for us. It is the energy of need that draws it out.

"The answer could come from any number of sources. It could come from a friend who decides to drop by on the spur of the moment. It could come during a lecture, or at a group discussion. The answer might even come from an unlikely source, a television documentary, for example.

"We might capture our answer on a piece of paper blowing across a parking lot; or discover it in a magazine. A billboard at a rapid-transit station might catch our attention in passing. As Simon and Garfunkel pointed out in their song: 'The words of the prophets are written on the subway walls.'

"Writing is an excellent way to tap into self-knowledge. Something magical happens when we sit down in front of a blank screen or an empty sheet of paper. We're often amazed at how much we *know*.

"Flashes of inspiration also convey self-knowledge, as do dreams. For this reason, many people choose to contemplate on a subject just before retiring for the night. Often our answers are there to greet us when we first wake up in the morning.

"In a nutshell, when we use our imagination to gain an understanding, whether mundane or cosmic, we are attaching our own electronic keynote to the idea. It is then filed away as self-knowledge. At this point, the ego takes inventory of all related belief patterns in the Seedbed and transmutes them, every last one. When we need the answer, it comes. That simple!

"It should always be remembered that outside information—any knowledge coming to us from sources other than ourselves—should be viewed simply as seed material for contemplation. It is up to us to establish our own self-knowledge. Reading the works of others, no matter how uplifting, has the same effect as repeating affirmations. The information is screened by the Belief System to ensure that it conforms to the parameters we have created. This is why we need to reacquaint ourselves with our abandoned gift of God, the imagination."

M: "If I'm understanding this right, we can take someone else's ideas and make them our own by putting them into pictures. Is this correct?" The Chief confirmed this with a mute nod.

"What is the difference between imagination and visualization?"

JR: "It's a difference of intent. Let's use a flashlight as an example. If we shine the light toward the heavens on a dark night, we can see the beam spread out. In like fashion, through contemplation we can shine the spotlight of our attention into the starry realm of archetypal ideas to establish self-knowledge and transmute the Seedbed. This is using the imagination.

"Now, when we focus the flashlight on an object on the ground, the beam gets smaller as the light intensifies. Similarly, we can use concentrated visualization to manifest our wants and desires. The vibrations of our thoughts are slowed down and coalesce into mineral form. We can use the same flashlight to accomplish two different purposes. Think of it this way: Imagination/contemplation/self-knowledge on one hand; visualization/concentration/manifestation on the other."

M: "What is the first step in establishing self-knowledge?"

JR: "The first and only step is contemplation—putting the idea or concept into picture form. Here's an exercise you can try: Sit in silence with your eyes closed. Your feet should be touching the floor. Take a few deep breaths and sing the word HU (pronounced HYOO), or any other word that feels right. Shortly you will begin to relax as your mind clears and the distractions of the day are left behind.

"You can also lie on your bed if you prefer; however, the *Ki* energy that flows upward from the center of the Earth and up through your body won't be as strong. Ki (also called *Qi* or *Chi* in Chinese) is a crystalline energy field that enables our thoughts to be divided into opposites in a light wave.[2] Hawaiian Kahunas and martial artists alike use Ki energy for a variety of purposes including fire walking, self-protection, and telepathic communication.

"Once you're sufficiently relaxed, direct the Ki energy upward through your body using your breath and imagination. In your mind's eye, see it flowing upward along the spine and neck until it enters your head. When this energy reaches the lower brain, it normally turns back and flows in the opposite direction. We can alter its course, however.

"Imagine two switches, one on each side of your head, at the temple area. With imaginary hands, flip these switches forward. The Ki energy will now flow into the frontal lobe of the brain and into the third eye, located at the level of the eyebrows in the center of the forehead, about an inch and a half back.

"Now, this is the fun part." From past discussions, the Chief knew I was a Star Trek fan; thus the exercise he suggested was appropriate. "Imagine that your third eye is the bridge of the U.S.S. Enterprise. As you enter the room, use all your senses to set the scene. Listen for sounds. Is music playing in the background? Is there an electrical hum? Is someone talking? Who else is present? Do you smell roses? If so, where are they located? What color is the carpet? Is there food? (an important question). If so, how does it taste? The captain's chair awaits. Is it adjustable? How does it feel? Is it leather? Is it warm? Has someone been sitting there before you?

"Turn your attention to the large viewing screen and the universe of stars beyond. Now, with a wave of your hand sweep the stars aside. Replace them with an empty stage with a brilliant spotlight shining down from above. This represents the spotlight of your attention, your *conscious light of intelligence*. It's important to include yourself in the scene, as well. You can do this in one of two ways. You can project into it, or you can remain in the captain's chair and watch an image of yourself perform on stage.

"Start with something familiar. If you want to explore the concept of love, for example, you can recall the affection you felt for your first girlfriend. See yourself holding hands. Revisit your first kiss. Immerse yourself in the feeling of infatuation. Don't forget to include all five of your senses. Another image will follow.

"It might be a Christmas gift-giving scene with your parents. How is this love different than the love you felt for your girlfriend? You can call up pictures of friendships and beloved pets. Remember, you are not trying to get an answer at this point. You are simply holding your attention on the concept of love so your Higher Self can gather information. It will then be filed away as self-knowledge in your causal mind.

"Even though we might be seeking self-knowledge on the highest form of love, Divine Love, we need to start with something familiar. In other words, we have to start where we are, not where we'd like to be."

The Chief rose from the bench and stretched his arms above his head. "What do you say we head back to the cabin and build a bonfire? We can roast some corn and potatoes."

My stomach had been growling for two hours. I could definitely put myself in *that* picture. After dinner I would ask the Chief about the Golden Formula.

*   *   *

> The more aware you become,
> the more you shed from day to day
> what you've learned
> so that your mind is always fresh
> and uncontaminated
> by previous conditioning.
>
> – Bruce Lee
> *Tao of Jeet Kune Do*[3]

THE MIRROR OF LIFE
AND THE GOLDEN FORMULA

A spiritual teacher was once asked the question, "How does one reach mastership?"

"By taking ten thousand little steps," was his reply. Now, more than ever, each tiny step counts. The wonders of modern technology do nothing to prepare us for the changes ahead. They serve only to distract us from our contemplations. It's much easier to pass a couple of mindless hours after work in front of the television watching a fictional family, than to examine our own lives. But with 2012 just around the corner, a few steps not wasted can truly make a difference.

It is the unspoken goal of every individual that embodies on a form world to learn to qualify his life-force energy to express love. Without establishing self-knowledge, or true understanding, this cannot be done. This is why masters generally advise their students to first seek understanding. At every step, it is understanding that opens the next door through which we must pass on our journey home to the Ocean of Light.

*   *   *

A recent windstorm had covered the Chief's back lawn with a brown blanket of brittle oak leaves. He'd spent several hours the day before raking them into a pile and gathering fallen branches. We threw in some larger pieces of dried oak for good measure. While the fledgling fire crackled and popped, we wrapped corn in aluminum foil and prepared a fresh salad of lettuce, tomatoes, carrots, scallions, and sprouts. The potatoes would go in the fire unwrapped. There is nothing better than the smoky flavor of potatoes baked in an oak bonfire.

While we waited for the fire to produce a hotbed of coals, we pulled up a couple of recliners. A game of musical chairs ensued, as the cool west wind shifted direction time and again. Dancing smoke promised a stinging penalty of burning eyes for the slow of foot. Even so, our discussion of the Belief System continued.

JR: "When Albert Einstein was asked how he discovered the Theory of Relativity he is said to have replied, 'I thought about it all the time.' We can assume that he used pictures to establish self-knowledge on the subject. This is how we must approach the Belief System, as well. We must contemplate on it.

"Johannes Brahms, the famous composer, also found inspiration for his masterpieces during contemplation, as did Beethoven. Measure for measure, the finished work was revealed to Brahms in these semi-trance states. He claimed that during these contemplative sessions, he came in contact with 'higher powers.' Divine vibrations not only filled his body with ecstasy, they formed pictures in his mind's eye.

"Had the saints of old understood the ego, their struggle to eliminate the Seedbed would have been much easier. They believed, however, that the ego was 'of the devil.' They failed to understand its role and modus operandi. In an attempt to kill it, they subjected themselves to many unnecessary austerities and physical hardships. This actually delayed their success.

"In extreme cases the ego can perish. This can happen during times of great stress, like the death of a loved one. But then a new ego must be created by the higher mind to replace it."

When my mother translated from this life, it felt like a part of me had died with her. I wondered if this had been my ego.

JR: "In our contemplations of the Seedbed, we will eventually come to the *Law of Proximity,* also called the *Mirror of Life.* This is a very important discovery. **In unconscious obedience to this law, each person who comes within our sphere of influence (50 feet) must reflect back to us the contents of our Belief System.**[1]

"One day at a supermarket I noticed a woman struggling to open her car door. She was having difficulty because she was holding two large grocery bags. I offered to help, but she politely turned me down. She didn't want to trouble a stranger with her problem. My first thought was: 'This woman has difficulty receiving from others.' Coincidentally, this incident happened at a time when I was contemplating on the Mirror of Life.

"After reviewing my encounter with this woman, however, I came to a second conclusion, this one about myself: '*I* am the one having difficulty receiving. *I* don't want to bother others with *my* problems.' I realized that the universe had brought this woman into my life to mirror a judgment that I was unconsciously holding. I did some more investigating.

"A man in a restaurant complained to me about 'all the rude drivers on the road these days.' Other drivers would routinely cut in front of him without signaling. When this man needed to change lanes in heavy traffic, no one would let him in.

"I listened politely, silently assessing the situation. My driving experience was just the opposite of this stranger's. I couldn't remember the last time I'd been treated unkindly. Therefore, I surmised that this man was meeting a reflection of his own abusive attitude on his daily commute. Although he didn't realize it, life was doing him a favor by bringing this to his attention.

"From that day forward, whenever I was presented with a problem I would ask myself, 'Is this problem common to everyone?' If the answer was 'no,' I would regard it as a reflection of my own Belief System." [The Chief once called this introspective practice *Sat Shatoiya,* the Way of True Reflection.]

"When we criticize others for their impatience, we are really judging our own reflection...and we are telling the world that *we* are the impatient one! Twenty-five hundred years ago the Essenes wrote about this in the *Dead Sea Scrolls.* They observed that 'events in the world around us mirror our own beliefs.'[2]

"We might say to ourselves 'I'm not impatient,' or, 'I'm not jealous.' But either of these qualities could be a carryover from other lifetimes. If something bothers us about another person, it is a sure indication that the problem is actually ours. Even if the person is acting in a manner that is driving us crazy, we can still thank him for bringing this quality within ourselves to light. If this annoying quality weren't present in our own Seedbed, then his behavior wouldn't have bothered us in the least. Even more likely, we wouldn't have attracted this person to us to begin with.

"The Mirror of Life also brings us a reflection of trapped emotions, ones we have refused to acknowledge and feel in the past. As we discussed earlier, when a thought is divided in a light wave, the quality of that thought determines the emotion that is generated when the energy of desire is also set in motion. When we suppress emotions, we cheat ourselves of the full experience. Furthermore, this bottled-up energy must one day be released. This is where the Mirror of Life fits in.

"As an example, let's say that we unconsciously harbor suppressed feelings of guilt left over from breaking up with our first girlfriend. At that time in our life, a lack of understanding resulted in thoughts that created this guilt. To complicate things, instead of feeling it, releasing it, and then moving on to the next moment, we suppressed these painful feelings. A portion of our personal power is tied up in these engrams from the past.

"These suppressed feelings of guilt will continue to mirror themselves in subsequent experiences until the original feeling is released. In other words, a pattern develops.

"We forget to invite cousin Edna to the wedding. We leave the dog at home alone for the holidays. We stay out late playing pool with the boys when our wife is sick at home. Any of these experiences could trigger and release the original feelings of guilt. If we continue to hold them in, however, the universe will bring us more powerful experiences.

"One day we accidentally burn down the house. Now we *really* feel guilty! At last the original emotional charge that we suppressed so long ago is released. Had we only allowed ourselves to feel guilty about our first breakup, all of these subsequent experiences could have been avoided.

"Until we are aware of this mirroring process, we will attack those who say and do things that trigger these painful emotions. We will blame them for being insensitive, instead of expressing our gratitude for their service. Life brings us precious gifts in tattered boxes, but we toss them aside unappreciatively, missing the jewels within. Once we gain understanding, however, we will welcome all of life's gifts with open arms.

"Because Earth is opening up to the fourth dimension, all trapped emotions vibrating at the lowest frequencies must be released. These emotions include anger, sadness, jealousy, guilt, and rage. We can also include feelings associated with abandonment and rejection. There is one more, however, that tops the list. That emotion is *fear*. Humanity is holding fear in staggering amounts." [Terrorism may be an outward reflection of trapped fear.] The Chief's normally soothing voice took on an ominous tone. "...And that fear must be released or transmuted by love prior to our dimensional shift!"[3]

M: "How do we know if our painful feelings are anchored in the past or belong to the present?"

JR: "It really doesn't matter if they're current or ancient. In either case, we can only release them in the present moment. That is our only point of power. But once we gain an understanding of the Belief System and the Mirror of Life, we will react differently to events. We will then set thoughts in motion that produce feelings of kindness and compassion, not the 'lower-vibration' emotions. If at that time we still feel guilty, however, we can assume it is a carryover from the past.

"Another important point, Michael. When we release these trapped feelings, we must not judge them as being good or bad. We simply release them. Too often we view ourselves as 'bad people' when we discover trapped feelings of anger left over from our past. First of all, we're not our thoughts or feelings, and secondly, we are not the same person today that we were when these emotions were generated. How different our reality would be if we would only stop judging.

"Judge not, the scriptures tell us. But they don't tell us 'how *not* to judge.'" The Chief paused to stir the fire, prompting my obvious question.

M: "Then how do we keep from judging?"

JR: The Chief took a moment before answering. "As we grow deeper in our understanding and appreciation of the universe, our consciousness will expand. We will move from *thinking* into *knowing,* and later into *being.* Many times in the human consciousness we put the cart before the horse. We say to ourselves, 'I must be humble in order to reach mastership,' when in truth, humility is the *result* of spiritual awakening. We think that we must drop certain behavior, like judging, in order to attain perfection. But in truth, we are already perfect in every way. The more we realize this, the less judgmental we will be.

"Furthermore, judgment requires opposites: good/bad, pretty/ugly, etc. In the realms of Pure Being, there are no opposites for comparison. For now, however, to keep from judging we can *evaluate* the action, but we must *bless* the individual involved. Once we know who we are, we will also know who he is—another White Fire Being exercising his gift of choice. We may not like that choice from where we stand, but we can still evaluate the action objectively and give him our blessing as we go about our business.

"Even in the case of horrible crimes, it is possible to stay balanced. When an armed gunman opens fire at a fast food restaurant killing several children, for example, we tend to despise the shooter and feel sympathy for the innocent children. Only when we understand how the universe operates can we free ourselves from condemnation and sympathy.

"In truth, each player in the drama agreed to participate in the experience prior to their incarnation. Perhaps the gunman had judged others harshly in the past. He might have signed on for the current experience to learn how it feels to be harshly judged and resented. The individuals now embodied as children likely took the life of a child in a prior incarnation. To satisfy the Law of Cause and Effect, their own lives were cut short this time around.

"In this example, the gunman wasn't 'evil,' nor were the children 'good.' They were both willing participants in the dance of life, a dance that sometimes appears cruel to the untrained observer.

"Just as an awakened master will never judge another because he understands the nature of the universe, he will not blame another for his own problems. Self-responsibility is a high mark of mastership.

"If we view ourselves as victims of circumstance, the Mirror of Life will faithfully bring us experiences to confirm our view. We will walk this Earth with our head hung low looking for sympathy and miss the grandeur of the stars. And of course we will attract plenty of accommodating people who are unaware of the mechanics of the universe to further support our 'poor me' attitude.

"The victim consciousness leads to further problems: self-pity, blame, complaining, and misplaced anger. Once we understand the Law of Cause and

Effect and our role as creators, however, we will take responsibility for the events in our life. We will cease to think of ourselves as victims."

When I was going to college someone broke into my car and stole my stereo. I told the Chief that I still felt angry about it, and was having trouble forgiving the perpetrator. "Are you telling me that we should bless those who steal from us?"

JR: "It *can* be done. Had it happened to me, I would have looked upon the individual as an agent of the Lords of Karma rather than as a thief. No doubt there were other cars parked on the same block. Since the individual had chosen to break into mine, I would have assumed that I had drawn the experience to myself. Perhaps I had attracted the experience to release pent-up anger. Or perhaps I had stolen something in the past and my thoughts were now being called in for balancing.

"After feeling and releasing any trapped emotions, I might have said something like, 'Oh, so that's how it feels to be robbed!' Or I might have asked myself, 'What can I learn from this experience?' From this perspective, I could evaluate the experience with objectivity, then bless the individual for his part in the drama."

M: "Then you would forgive the person?"

JR: "No. There would be no need to forgive him. To do so would presuppose that I had been wronged and had been a victim. No one is ever wronged. Look at it this way, we learn our lessons by experiencing both sides of the coin, so to speak. We learn what it is like to be a thief; then we learn how it feels to be robbed. The same is true when we harm others.

"We can learn what it feels like to be harmed in one of two ways. We can experience it as a physical event, or we can experience it in our imagination. Either way will work. Once we've learned the lesson, it is then filed away in our causal body as self-knowledge. It will not be necessary to draw further experiences of harm to ourselves.

"When we have fully experienced the concept of stealing, then we won't have to lock our car when we go to the mall anymore. We won't have to lock up our skis when we break for lunch at the ski resort. The only time we'll need to lock anything is when we get a strong inner nudge to do so.

"When we understand the lesson of harm, then we'll become invincible. We will walk without fear. Best of all, once we understand the reciprocal nature of learning, we will never have to judge others as perpetrators or as victims. We can skip the misplaced anger, blame, and sympathy."

M: "Do spiritual masters ever feel guilty?"

JR: "No. First of all, a master never creates a situation where another is harmed. If circumstances beyond his control should allow this to happen, however, he would look upon himself simply as a vehicle for helping the individual concerned clean up his Belief System or release trapped feelings."

M: "Speaking of cleaning up the Belief System, where does the Golden Formula fit in?"

JR: "The Golden Formula is a powerful four-step approach to problem solving. It consists of **imagination**, **self-responsibility**, **understanding**, and lastly, **release**. It is really a quick-reference guide to cleaning up the Belief System. [A template of the Golden Formula appears at the end of this chapter.]

"To recap, our Higher Self will bring the next thing we need to work on to our attention. This will be whatever is currently giving us physical discomfort, mental anguish, or emotional pain.

"We start by couching this problem in picture form using the imagination. It is important to note that we are not trying to solve the problem at this point. We are simply holding our attention on it so our Higher Self can view it. As usual, we start with a familiar image and let others unfold naturally. Spend as much time as necessary (10 to 15 minutes minimum). Acknowledge, feel, and release any trapped feelings that come up. [By saying "I love you," "I'm sorry," "please forgive me," and "thank you," we can facilitate this release and free up trapped will power.]

"Next, we must take absolute responsibility for creating the problem. We cannot blame anyone else for our difficulties. How can we release a problem that is not ours? If harm is being done to us at present, it is because we have harmed others in the past. These thoughts are now being called in for balancing.

"We must understand both our role as creators, and the nature of the Belief System. We must understand that our Higher Self has brought the problem to our attention because it is time to be balanced. We may never know the actual source of our problem. It is enough to know that the true cause lies in our past thoughts, not our current thinking. We must also understand that objects of nature such as alcohol, caffeine, and meat have no power of their own. It is our belief that empowers them.

"It is the combination of self-responsibility and understanding that balances the thoughts and transmutes the Belief System. In other words, the lesson has been learned. The information is then filed away in our causal body as self-knowledge. Gratitude is the grounding principle that anchors the solution into our life.

"Finally, we must release the problem. This is generally the hardest part. Most people look for results too quickly. It is important to remember that the problem may persist for awhile, until the body gets 're-wired' to accommodate our new belief pattern.

"Another temptation is to re-think the problem—to release it, then take it back. We can use switch-words like 'It's okay' or 'I love you' when our attention drifts back to the problem. Some find it helpful to run through the Golden Formula again.

"In addition to switch-words, we can also use pictures to formalize the release. We can 'white-out' the problem in our mind, for example. Here's another powerful technique: When we come to the release step, we can visualize a pair of large, cloud-like hands. We gently place the problem in these cupped hands and see them close in around it. We can say something like, 'Well, that's done,' as we watch the hands dissipate in the clear, blue sky.

"After using the Golden Formula template a few times, we may find that we no longer need it. Once we understand our part in creating the problem, we will automatically take responsibility for it. Once we understand that objects of nature have no power of their own, we won't have to repeat that section over and over, either, will we?" The Chief shook his head for me.

"By and large, the only persistent challenge for most of us will be the release part. Perhaps this will shed light on the process. Picture the Seedbed as a giant pyramid with our destructive patterns settled near the bottom (Fig. 5). In our contemplations, we add bits of self-knowledge to the top. Over time they filter down through the pyramid, pushing the old patterns out the bottom when we no longer need them.

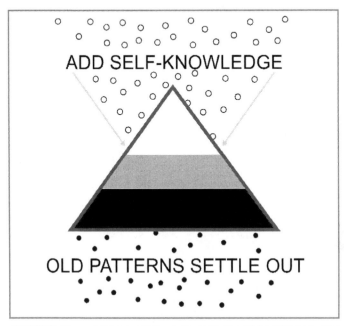

FIGURE 5: PYRAMID OF SELF-KNOWLEDGE

"Some of these patterns occupy many layers in the Belief System. Meat eating and alcohol are two examples. Countless lifetimes of repetitive thinking have left deep grooves that manifest as habits. We can't expect for these habits to drop away overnight, although in some cases they do. It could take months or even years for desires associated with powerful belief patterns to cease. In the meantime, we must be confident enough in our own self-knowledge to ignore the outer circumstances while the filtering down and re-wiring process takes place. Our patience and faith will undoubtedly be tested."

*　　　　*　　　　*

A little after eight-thirty we removed the charred potatoes from the smoldering coals. The Chief brought out some sea salt and butter, along with some chilled apple juice. It was well worth the wait. Although many years have passed, the memory of those smoky baked potatoes still makes my mouth water.

THE GOLDEN FORMULA
for Eliminating Problems, Fears, and Addictions

IMAGINATION

Use the imagination to put the problem into picture form. This bypasses the sensory mind and Belief System. You should also include yourself in the picture (and your spiritual guide if you choose). We are simply holding the attention on the problem, not trying to solve it. It doesn't have to be an accurate representation. Take your time. Acknowledge, feel, and release any trapped emotional pain that comes up. Do this without judgment.

SELF-RESPONSIBILITY (repeat:)

I take absolute responsibility for creating the problem, and accept any solution that comes into my life as the workings of my Higher Self.

UNDERSTANDING (repeat:)

I understand that the problem is in my life at this time because it is something that needs balancing now. (The energy of need draws the solution.)

I understand that the true cause of the problem lies in my past thoughts, not my current thinking.

I understand that _____ is only an object of nature and has no power of its own.

(Look for cause and effect relationships.) Example:

I understand that _____ is doing harm to me now because I have harmed others in the past.

RELEASE (repeat:)

I hereby release the problem and call upon my Higher Self to transmute my Belief System to reflect my new understanding. SO BE IT! (It isn't necessary to know the root cause of the problem.)

Use your imagination: Feel the joy and gratitude as you celebrate your newfound freedom. (Gratitude is the grounding principle that anchors the solution into your life.)

NOTES: Don't re-think the problem. Use the switch-words "It's okay" or "I love you." You can also "white-out" the problem in your mind's eye, or run the problem through the Golden Formula again. The symptoms may continue for a time until the physical body gets re-wired.

91

THE MECHANICS OF NON-RESISTANCE

I spent the following weekend, Thanksgiving, in front of the television set watching football as I did every year. Although much has changed in my life since 1987, it is a tradition that I honor to this day. At that time, however, I still believed that Lee Harvey Oswald had acted alone in assassinating JFK... and I still believed the six o'clock news was a fair representation of the day's events. I even admired and respected our elected officials. After all, they were looking out for our best interest! Alas, how naïve I was.

Once we are aware of the myriad deceptions used by those who deal in the Kal, or negative power, we can set about reclaiming our freedom. Information about how we've been controlled is readily available, but most people scoff at the idea of conspiracies. This is a testament to the successful mass indoctrination that begins at birth and leaves us trembling at the grave.

As one person retorted, "If there *was* a conspiracy, don't you think we'd have heard about it on the evening news or read about it in the papers?" Rather than explain further or argue the point, I respected her opinion. But I thought to myself, "What aspect of society today is not without its closely guarded secrets?"

In 1913 President Woodrow Wilson alluded to "the powers that be" in his book, *The New Freedom:*

> Since I entered politics, I have chiefly had men's views confided to me privately. Some of the biggest men in the U.S., in the field of commerce and manufacturing, are afraid of somebody, are afraid of something. They know that there is a power somewhere so organized, so subtle, so watchful, so interlocked, so complete, so pervasive, that they had better not speak above their breath in condemnation of it.[1]

So how has this secret cabal remained hidden? According to Dr. John Coleman, author of *The Committee of 300*, all three major television networks can trace their beginnings to RCA. RCA, the Radio Corporation of America, was formed by General Electric, Westinghouse, Morgan Guarantee and Trust (acting on behalf of the British crown), and American Fruits back in 1919 as a British intelligence center. The networks were, and still are, dominated by British intelligence.[2]

But surely my friend can sip her café latte at Starbucks and trust what she reads in the morning paper? Not likely. According to the congressional record of 1917, two years earlier J.P. Morgan and other captains of industry recruited twelve men high up in the newspaper world. These twelve men were charged with the covert task of securing controlling interests in the most influential newspapers in the United States.

Initially they selected 179 newspapers, but finally eliminated all but twenty-five of the greatest ones. They found that by purchasing these twenty-five papers they could control the content of the daily press throughout America! They then furnished each paper with an editor who could properly supervise and edit information to accommodate the interests of those operating behind the scenes.[3]

To those holding power, a captive world is much easier to manage if the masses remain ignorant of who they are, and how they are being controlled. Better to keep the people entertained than have them thinking for themselves. Better a nation of consumers than a nation of unruly God-Realized beings. Rather than freedom, let the people cry for more government hand-outs—much less dangerous.

We may rightly complain that we are the most controlled and manipulated society in history, but what can we find of value in this "tattered box?" Is there anything to be learned from this experience?

To fully understand a lesson, we must experience both polarities. To fully appreciate the value of freedom, it is essential to understand what freedom is not. What better setting could there be for the study of opposites than 21st century Earth?

As we wake up to the fact that we are being manipulated, the biggest challenge for us will not be to uncover the magnitude of this control and reclaim our power. It will be to withhold judgment. Once we have established self-knowledge on the true nature of the universe, however, we will cease to view the performers in this cosmic drama as either good or bad. We will free ourselves from the subtlest, yet most dangerous, self-imposed control of all: judgment.

Prior to the Chief's discourse on non-resistance, I thought it might be helpful to include a couple of examples of control. In both cases, vast numbers of people have been affected. Hundreds of other examples can be found on the Internet, in alternative newspapers, and on talk radio.[4] Some, due to their unbelievable nature, afford those working with the negative current a blanket of security.

[The following excerpts express views held by their original authors and are reprinted here without verification. They have been paraphrased for brevity.]

Nicolai Tesla and Free Energy. Bielek, Al, 1996 lecture. Bielek, a key participant in "The Philadelphia Experiment," describes Tesla's accomplishments.

Nicolai Tesla was Serbian born, but immigrated to the United States in 1884. He was the father of the alternating current, as well as many other life-changing innovations like the Tesla Coil. Forty patents have been registered in his name; yet few references to him can be found in history books, for his discoveries have been subverted and information about his life, suppressed. Because of this man's genius, those working behind the scenes have allegedly had complete control of the weather since the 1970's.

The inventor once reported that he was in contact with beings from "off-planet," while living in Colorado Springs, Colorado, and later in his New York City laboratory. How this may have benefited his work is not known.

Tesla is credited with designing the powerful electromagnetic coils used on the *Eldridge,* the ship made invisible in the famed "Philadelphia Experiment." The movie by the same name is for the most part factual, with a few embellishments by the filmmakers. Tesla eventually left the Philadelphia Project when he correctly foresaw serious problems ahead for the crew-members of the ship. It is evident from this gesture that he was a man of principle, with the betterment of the world in mind.

In 1906 the Wardenclyffe Tower was constructed on Long Island. A year before its completion, Tesla walked into the office of J.P. Morgan, the financier of the project. Tesla announced that he intended to use the Wardenclyffe Tower to provide free power to every-one! A surprised J.P. Morgan responded indignantly, "You mean to tell me that you can stick a rod in the ground and an antenna in the air, and generate free power forever?" Tesla answered in the affirmative.

J.P. Morgan said something like "Don't call me, I'll call you," and immediately cut off all funding. The Wardenclyffe Tower was never used as planned. It was dynamited in 1914.[5]

Royal Rife's Cure for Cancer. Lynes, Barry, *The Cancer Cure That Worked.*

Royal Rife was born in 1888, and translated from this life in 1971. In 1933 he created a microscope consisting of 6,000 parts that was capable of magnifying objects 60,000 times their normal size. He became the first human being to see a living virus. The modern electron microscope instantly kills everything beneath it. Rife's did not.

Because of this, he was able to determine the specific electromagnetic signature of most diseases. Furthermore, he discovered that any disease could be painlessly eliminated with frequencies based on these signatures. These included herpes, polio, spinal meningitis, tetanus, influenza, and a great number of other dangerous disease organisms.

In 1934 the University of California appointed a Special Medical Research Committee to bring terminally ill cancer patients to Rife's clinic. The team of doctors and pathologists were to examine the patients after 90 days, providing any were still alive.

After the 90 days had passed, 86.5% of the patients had been completely cured. When Rife adjusted the treatment, the remaining 13.5% also responded within four weeks. *The total recovery rate was 100%.* Royal Rife was later honored at a banquet billed as "The End to All Disease." But by 1939 the same doctors and scientists were denying they had ever met Rife.

When news of his success spread, powerful forces attacked him. Morris Fishbein, who had acquired the entire stock of the AMA, the American Medical Association, sent an attorney to Rife's office with 'an offer he could not refuse.' Rife refused. Arthur Kendall, the Director of the Northwestern School of Medicine, who had worked with Rife on the cancer virus, accepted almost a quarter of a million dollars to suddenly 'retire' in Mexico. This was an exorbitant amount of money in the Depression.

Those making a fortune on the treatment of disease had no intention of letting Rife continue his work. [Today the treatment of a single cancer patient averages over $400,000.][6] The pharmaceutical industry purged his work from all their medical journals. Furthermore, pieces of his universal microscope were stolen from his lab along with photographs, film, and written records. The police illegally confiscated the remainder of Rife's 50 years of research.

The magnitude of such suppression boggles the mind. Without the benefits of Rife's work, by 1960 the casualties from cancer alone exceeded the carnage from all of America's wars. In 1989 it was estimated that 40% of all Americans would succumb to cancer. Today the percentage is much higher. Meanwhile, the American Cancer Society, the Salk Foundation, and many other institutions collect hundreds of millions of dollars every year for diseases for which cures existed in the 1930's![7]

Rife's frequency generators are needed now more than ever with the advent of AIDS and other "designer viruses." Fortunately, a few humanitarian doctors and engineers have reconstructed his frequency machines and have kept his dream alive.

*   *   *

The week after Thanksgiving I met the Chief at a local coffee shop around 11:00 a.m. He'd called a few days before to ask if I'd like to meet for a late breakfast since he'd be in town running some errands. I was anxious to quiz him about a disturbing dream I'd had a few nights earlier.

The restaurant was crowded, even for a Saturday. A harried waitress finally bustled up to our table with a coffee pot in one hand and water in the other. The Chief ordered a vegetarian omelet and a side of sourdough toast. I followed suit, but opted for coffee. Only one other customer in our section besides the Chief had passed on the steaming brew.

While many consider eggs "off limits," I allowed myself the luxury of three or four a week. The Chief, however, consumed all the eggs he wanted. Evidently he hadn't heard about the famous study. I took it upon myself to enlighten him about the danger of eggs. He listened politely as I explained how eating too many eggs resulted in high cholesterol.[8] When I had finished, he asked me a question.

"Did you happen to catch the name of the 'health authority' responsible for the findings on eggs?" I shook my head "no," but assumed that it had been the AMA, or perhaps a public watchdog group.

"Would you believe the cereal companies? That's right, the cereal companies." The Chief smiled wryly. "They wanted to boost sales, so they stacked the deck against their rival, the poultry industry.

"They fed dried egg yolk powder, a form of oxidized cholesterol, to a group of test mice. Not surprisingly, their cholesterol levels were a bit high, especially since the servings were approximately 100 times a normal mouse-sized portion. In other words, they super-sized it! The cholesterol in eggs is actually beneficial to the human body. It is the body's natural 'clay,' part of the cell survival system. It is responsible for regulating the flow of water through the cell membrane. High cholesterol levels stem largely from dehydration, not eggs—which, by the way, are also a good source of protein. In fact, the protein in eggs is the standard against which all other sources are measured.

"Like some big businesses, whenever those in power want to guide the masses in a particular direction that suits their purpose, they do it covertly. They decide on an objective, then create a problem that can only lead to one solution—the one that fulfills their objective. In the case of eggs, the objective of the cereal companies was 'increased sales.' To accomplish this, they artificially created a problem. They convinced a large number of people, through deceit, that their competition's product was unhealthy. They then promoted the 'desired solution' in a fear-based advertising blitz: 'Skip the high-cholesterol eggs. Eat more cereal.' Bingo, their sales increased.

"Gun control is another example of mass manipulation. Before any country is taken over, its citizens must be disarmed. This is what happened in Hitler's Germany. The people were naïve. They believed it could never happen in *their* country. Of course the state-controlled news media promulgated the illusion. A similar naiveté exists in these United States. Australia is one of many countries presently losing its fight to keep and bear arms. But don't expect to hear anything about this on the evening news.

"Let me ask you this, Michael. If you wanted to exercise total control, how would you go about confiscating every gun in a country? Could you do it with the blessings of its citizens? Would they, in fact, beg you to take their guns away?" I couldn't see how this could happen.

JR: "It would be a simple matter if you were cold and unscrupulous. You could promote random acts of violence in schools and in public areas. You could make the streets and playgrounds unsafe. With sophisticated mind control technology like *Project Monarch,* the oldest and largest CIA mind control program, this could easily be done.[9] When kids began killing other kids, there would be a public outcry: 'Please, take away our guns!'

"Does this problem-reaction-solution scenario sound too horrific to be possible? Would those influenced by the Kal Power actually stoop to murdering children to accomplish their objective, world domination? The answer to both questions is 'yes'...and when those holding power come to take our guns, most people will thank them for it."

M: "How can we resist this takeover?"

JR: "A good question. But it is not the outer circumstances that must change. It is our Belief System.

Remember the Law of Proximity? Those who come within fifty feet of us must reflect the contents of our Seedbed. In a similar vein, leaders are a reflection of the consciousness of the people they represent. If we could vote the current leaders out of office, their replacements would be nearly identical in every way. Leaders simply reflect the belief patterns of the group consciousness. They are not the problem. They are the symptom.

"In 1849 Henry David Thoreau wrote in *Civil Disobedience:*

> I heartily accept the motto, "That government is best which governs least;" and I should like to see it acted up to more rapidly and systematically. Carried out, it finally amounts to this, which also I believe—"That government is best which governs not at all;" and when men are prepared for it, that will be the kind of government they will have.[10]

"So, how do we prepare for this ideal government, one that governs not at all? It is actually quite simple. We get our own house in order. Then we won't attract a negative reflection of our Seedbed in the form of a controlling government. As the populace becomes more responsible, the government will reflect this, as well. Ultimately Thoreau's vision of 'non-government' will come to fruition.

"Now, a word about resistance. When Christ said, 'Resist not evil,' few people understood what he meant. He was referring to the *Law of Non-Resistance*. Whenever we resist anything in the universe, we give it power. Good cannot resist evil. It becomes that which it opposes. The energy slides down the polarity shaft of the light wave and strengthens that which is being resisted. It is no longer good.

"Evil can use any means at its disposal to oppose good. But it must rely on the resistance furnished by its opposition for its energy. Evil, if not resisted, must fall away of its own accord. It must go into the voidance phase of creation.

"Knowing this, the Kal will often set up counter-organizations for the purpose of promoting resistance. This has a two-fold effect. It generates energy for carrying out its agenda, and reveals the identities of those who oppose it.

"Lastly, when we resist evil we must first judge it as evil. Now that we understand the nature of the Seedbed and the Law of Proximity, we can trace evil to its source. It is our own Belief System! All the great sages have taught, 'Judge not, lest you be judging that which is within thine own Soul.'"[11]

It was nearing noon and the lunch crowd was starting to trickle in. Behind the counter the waitress poured a pitcher of beer for a customer. As the foam overflowed onto the counter below, my recent dream came to mind.

In the dream I'd found myself staring into the eyes of a jaguar. The animal was sleek and black, with a sapphire-blue collar draped about its neck. Playfully, we chased each other around the boxing ring we occupied. When we grew tired, the black jaguar would lay his head upon the top rope and purr contentedly as I stroked his head.

But when it came time for me to go, a dramatic change came over the animal. As I made my way across the canvas I heard a faint growl from behind. It became louder and more threatening as I reached for the rope. To my surprise, when I turned about, the beautiful jaguar had transformed into a different creature altogether. His once sleek fur was now dull-orange. Patches of fur had fallen out due to some disease. Fur stood on end at the back of its neck. The jaguar's clear, blue eyes were now blood red. Saliva foamed from its exposed fangs, and dripped upon the canvas below.

Whenever I would stop, the jaguar would relax. But each time I made the slightest attempt to go, it would growl more menacingly. To leave the ring would be dangerous, for the black jaguar intended to hold me in its power forever. I awoke in a cold sweat and puzzled over the meaning of the vivid dream most of the following day.

Now, as I watched the foam drip from the frosty glass of beer, I understood. Alcohol had been my friend for many years, but now the relationship had changed. As time had gone by, my dark friend had demanded more and more of my attention. The dream was showing me that the jaguar was not my friend. He was my captor. I told the Chief about the dream and asked him for advice.

"Does the Law of Non-Resistance also apply to addictions?"

JR: "Yes, it does. The more we resist, the stronger the hold of alcohol, drugs, or caffeine becomes. This is why most people fail in their battle against substance abuse. Some are able to stop temporarily, but unless they get to the root of the problem, it will eventually return. Denial doesn't work. It is a form of resistance.

"Alcoholism is not a disease. It is a social habit. The thought patterns that produce the craving for alcohol do not contain a disease factor. As illogical as it may sound, we should continue with our habit until the thought patterns have been balanced. This is what the blueprints in our Belief System call for. Once we balance the thoughts and release any trapped feelings, however, the electromagnetic current will be severed and our addiction will cease. In the meantime, we can practice moderation and focus on establishing healthy habits. This is also a good time to begin an inner cleansing program."

The Chief's position notwithstanding, some may choose a proactive approach to uncover the real problems masked by addiction. Once we become familiar with judgments and suppressed feelings, we can suspend the habit and see what comes up. We can acknowledge and express any past feelings of abandonment, sadness, guilt, or depression that may rise to the surface. Often these painful feelings from the past hide powerful judgments that can now be recognized and transmuted through new understandings. Once these have been removed, the habit may diminish or drop away altogether.

JR: "We can use the Golden Formula to establish self-knowledge on alcohol or any other addiction. By using pictures, we can focus our conscious light of intelligence on the subject. We must also take responsibility for our addiction. While our parents may have harbored similar beliefs, we did not inherit our dependence on alcohol from them. The desire stems from unbalanced thoughts in our own Belief System.

"Alcohol is a colorless, volatile liquid used as a medium in the making of pharmaceutical compounds. When consumed as a beverage, however, the spirit of the alcohol makes contact with desire in the blood and feeling in the nerves.[12] It can numb the senses and keep pain buried beneath the consciousness. But eventually we must experience what we have chosen to avoid—sadness, anger, loneliness, and fear. Often these feelings are associated with a loss of love, or a loss of control.

"Alcohol can appear to take on a life of its own. It can masquerade as a friend or dress as our enemy, depending on the thoughts that we hold in our Seedbed. Another important understanding is this: objects of nature, including alcohol, have no power of their own. We empower them according to our beliefs. Generally these beliefs originate in past incarnations and follow us from birth to the grave many times over before we learn the lesson and balance the thoughts.

"Often the guilt associated with drinking, smoking, or using drugs is more devastating than their actual use. Addiction is not a sentence to hell. It is but a single lesson in a broad curriculum. At some point over the course of our lifestream, each of us must face this challenge. We must learn that we are far more powerful than anything outside of ourselves.

"Once we release the problem, we should not look for results too quickly, if at all. We should give ourselves plenty of time for the new self-knowledge to transmute old belief patterns, and for the filtering down to take place. At some point, the desire 'not to drink' will outweigh the desire for alcohol. A desire for better health might shift this balance, for example.

"The more we work with the Golden Formula, the more faith we will have in the process. The less we will resist. We will be able to take our attention off unwanted habits, even though our outer circumstances may remain unchanged at first.

"Then one day, to our surprise, it will hit us—we haven't had a drink (or reached for a cigarette) in three weeks! The old patterns have been transmuted and the electromagnetic currents have been severed. Miraculously, the desire has vanished. We have eliminated the problem without resisting it."

*   *   *

On two separate occasions I've experienced the magic of non-resistance in my own life. In one instance I was working in a conventional water treatment facility as a night operator. Each morning the district engineer, a critical individual, would storm into the building intent on finding errors in my work. While he studied the 24-hour trends on the computer, I awaited his analysis with great trepidation.

But then I decided to change my approach. Rather than retreating to a corner to dream up possible explanations for my choices over the course of the night, I would simply walk to the window and start whistling. In a matter of moments the engineer would join me. We talked about rafting, motor homes, dogs, his retirement plans, and any number of other non-work-related topics. My water treatment decisions rarely came up.

Non-resistance also came in handy when a friend from high school responded to a book I'd sent him as a gift. In retrospect, the book had been much too controversial for my friend's orthodox way of thinking. Sending it had been a mistake. His letter was harshly critical.

After acknowledging my thoughtfulness, he proceeded to point out in the remainder of the letter how off base the New-Thought author had been. He pulled no punches in his critique. In closing, he stated that if the Bible was correct, and he believed that it was, then I was obviously headed straight for hell!

Two choices came to mind. I could fire back a letter in defense of the author's (and my) ideas, a rebuttal so to speak; or I could simply ignore the letter and let his argument go unchallenged.

Upon contemplation, however, I came up with a third option, an approach I've since learned to call *The High Road.* I sent him the kindest letter I'd ever written. I told him how much I had enjoyed hearing from him, and how much I appreciated his friendship. Nothing was said about our philosophical differences. Instead, I wrote of similarities, of common interests: movies, hiking, food, friends, and cars. I told him how much I looked forward to seeing him and his wife again when they returned home (he was a missionary in China at the time)...and I was sincere.

That letter changed at least one life. It was unexpected and unintended, but in that moment I experienced love in action. I remembered once again why love is such a valuable commodity in this world. True compassion is the most powerful force in the universe. It transmutes all lower frequencies.

My letter may have changed my friend's life, as well, I cannot say. But when he arrived Stateside, I was the first one he called.

              *   *   *

We are One
in the Circle of Life.
Love is All,
just open your heart.

– the author

AQUARIUS, THE "WATER-BEARER"

When I knocked on the cabin door the Sunday afternoon before Christmas, I was nursing a sore throat. It was nearing five-thirty, and a chilly east wind tugged at my coat collar while I waited in the twilight. At last the Chief's smiling eyes appeared in the tiny glass square in the top of the door.

Even though the temperature inside the cabin was around seventy, I set my sights on the fireplace hearth. Hearing my persistent cough, the Chief steeped the licorice root a bit longer than usual. He apologized for not having any angelica root to add to my tea as we settled in for a discussion.

M: "Will people still get sick in the Golden Age?"

JR: "The further we go into the Photon Belt, the less sickness we will create for ourselves. It will not happen as if by magic, however. It will be accomplished through a greater understanding of disease, and how we create our own reality.

"Poor health is the result of misqualified life-force energy. For example, when we constantly send out thoughts of anger, depression, low self-worth, and bitterness—in other words, negative thoughts—the blueprints used to build new cells in the body will reflect this disharmony. The universe sends out a symphony of love, nothing else. Destructive emotions generated by discordant thoughts are sour notes in the song of creation. The universe will move to destroy that which is out of balance with the Law of Love by releasing toxins. A cheerful, positive attitude is of inestimable worth.

"There is but one way to cure a disease or dissolve a condition: that is to remove the cause and core from the Belief System. We can use the Golden Formula for this, as well. Once removed, we will never suffer from that particular disease again. The thoughts that have caused it will have been upgraded, and the lesson learned.

"We can't automatically assume, however, that all health problems are the result of misqualified life-force energy. On rare occasions we will choose to take on a physical defect, disability, or an illness for the purpose of learning a particular lesson, or for helping another individual fulfill a karmic obligation. Some children born with severe mental disabilities, for example, are actually highly evolved Souls that have consciously chosen their 'needy' roles. Their gift of love and service might enable another Soul to repay a debt to life, or simply experience the joy of giving.

"Few areas in the Belief System are more convoluted than those dealing with health and sickness. Nowhere does the phrase 'garbage in—garbage out' seem more appropriate. Lifetimes of misinformation have left us crippled and in fear. Modern medicine has done little to right our ship. In fact, it has burned our lifeboats and has left us floundering in despair.

"Thoreau wrote: 'Trade curses everything it handles; and though you trade in messages from heaven, the whole curse of trade attaches to the business.'[1] Modern medicine is a trillion dollar a year business with its own agenda. Unfortunately, all too often that agenda promotes money and control rather than good health.

"Traditional doctors, however well meaning, are educated in schools heavily influenced (funded) by the pharmaceutical industry.[2] Information about the Belief System and the mechanics of creation are not part of their curriculum. Therefore, the true cause of disease is not taught. Modern medicine is largely a study of effects.

"Armed with incomplete information, doctors often treat symptoms instead of causes. Today a few traditional physicians are leaning toward a more holistic approach. This is a step in the right direction, but until doctors can view life from the higher perspective, they will continue to chase symptoms 'round and round' in the body.

"At best, synthetic drugs and pills can temporarily alleviate symptoms. But they also interfere with the body's natural process of healing and can weaken the immune system. Symptoms are not something to be 'cured.' They are generally the result of the body's attempt to correct numerous problems stemming from dehydration, toxicity, and pH imbalances."

M: "Can you give me an example of how doctors treat symptoms rather than causes?"

JR: The Chief thought for a moment, gazing out the window into the darkness. "A couple come to mind. When we eat an unhealthy diet loaded with processed sugars, artificial ingredients, and preservatives, damage is done to the body on the cellular level.[3] A call is sent out to the natural bacteria in our body to clean up a particular area in disrepair. Our temperature goes up, since added heat is needed by the cleanup crew to 'burn the garbage.' Other symptoms of 'a cold' appear: a runny nose, a sore throat, and a hacking cough.

"Responding to powerful beliefs in our Seedbed, we run to the doctor for immediate relief. He gives us antibiotics to fight the 'evil bacteria' that are attacking our body. Miraculously, the symptoms disappear. The cold or flu has been vanquished.

"The doctor goes home feeling fulfilled because he has helped another sick person; the pharmaceutical company is happy because it has sold another prescription of antibiotics; and we're happy because we think we've been cured. Unfortunately, however, the great casualty of this war is our long-term health. The repair work that would have fixed the problem has been interrupted, and our condition will continue to deteriorate.

"Here's another case. Our eyes itch and our nose is stuffy. We're having difficulty breathing. Again, we visit our physician. He tells us that high histamine levels are causing our problem—an accurate assessment.

"But he doesn't tell us *why* our histamine levels are high. Histamine is part of the body's 'drought management system.'[4] When we fail to drink an adequate amount of water, the body begins a rationing program. The brain is the first priority; anything left can be sent to the suburbs. (Our nose and eyes are part of the suburbs.)

"So the doctor, concentrating on the symptom instead of the cause, prescribes a strong anti-histamine. Our symptoms go away, so we think we've been cured. The doctor is fulfilled; the pharmaceutical company smiles all the way to the bank; but our health pays the price. We will continue to need stronger and stronger drugs to mask the symptoms of dehydration as our condition worsens.

"Salt is a natural anti-histamine. When dehydration becomes chronic, the body retains salt to help manage the drought conditions.⁵ Confusing the symptom with the problem, our physician tells us that we must avoid salt since our levels are high. Again, the body's efforts to heal itself are thwarted."

M: "Why don't people drink more water? None of my friends drink anywhere near the recommended amount: half their body weight in ounces of water per day."

JR: "I've given this a lot of thought. Even though people know to drink water, they come up with any number of excuses to explain why they don't: *Water is boring. It doesn't taste good. It smells like chlorine. I don't have a filter...* the list goes on and on. Many times they drink coffee or soda instead, even alcohol. All of these add to the problem. They dehydrate the body.

"When asked how much water they drink, most people furrow their brow and reply, 'I probably should drink more.' The only water some people consume is the water they use to wash down their medication. Many also believe that water in juice can answer the body's call for water. This is better than nothing, of course, but it's a poor substitute for the real thing. When water is combined with any other substance, it takes on the electronic keynote of that substance. The body interprets this new vibration as 'food.'

"I've come to the conclusion that we have to earn the right to drink water. We do this by upgrading the

Belief System. Water is the key to both maintaining and restoring good health. As long as we refuse to take responsibility for creating our maladies, however, the key will elude us. The desire for water will not be part of the blueprints sent down from the Seedbed.

"Notice that I didn't say water cured ill health. The cause of our problems is the misqualification of life-force energy through improper thinking. These thoughts, in turn, generate emotions that we deny, rather than feel. Once these thoughts are balanced using the Golden Formula and all pent-up emotional charge is released, the rebuilding of the body can begin. At this point, we will discover the magic of water. This is also the stage where herbs and good nutrition come in. These in and of themselves don't cure our problems, but they can be used to strengthen our immune system and provide good raw materials for rebuilding."

M: "Why is water so important?"

JR: "As we talked about earlier, water and air provide the two key ingredients necessary for maintaining our body and manifesting our thoughts: hydrogen and oxygen. Hydrogen compresses, hardens, and solidifies.[6] Oils and margarines are thickened by bubbling hydrogen through them. The solid consistency of these hydrogenated oils helps sell products, but they are difficult for the body to digest. Despite the negative publicity on butter, it is much better than its artificial counterparts.

"Oxygen softens and expands.[7] It removes the outer husk from the seed of life, the thought. Oxidation destroys the form, so the formless can materialize Itself again and again in different guises. Furthermore, when hydrogen and oxygen are combined with carbon and nitrogen, they form proteins.

Combined with carbon alone, they form carbohydrates.[8]

"Water also enables our subconscious mind and physical brain to communicate with the many systems of the body, the suburbs. Messages are transmitted over cords of light. Light travels on water. When messages can't get through to their destination, a signal is sent to the control center, the brain. It registers as pain. The water we drink restores the connection and the pain goes away. Of course we credit the pain medication, not the water, for our relief. Once again the giant pharmaceutical companies come out the winners."

M: "I've heard that highly-evolved spiritual masters can live solely on water. How is this possible?"

JR: "Everything is possible for an awakened being. Once we understand the nature of illusion, that everything here is a reflection of true causes that we control, we too will be able to create every vitamin, mineral, enzyme, or hormone with only two ingredients—air and water. But to live in this manner, we must first eliminate all contrary thoughts from the Belief System! Remember, everything is light. Who knows, once we break through the illusion of Maya, it may be possible to live on light alone!"

M: "Then cleaning out the Belief System must be the key to awakening."

JR: "That's a big part of it."

M: "I understand that we should drink a lot of water, but what kind of water should we drink?"

JR: "We should drink the highest-quality water we can find. Most cities use chlorine as their disinfectant. Chlorine is a deadly poison. Also called 'mustard gas,' it was used in WWII by the chemical warfare department. Chlorine can also combine with organic material in water to form harmful disinfection by-products, mainly trihalomethanes and haloacetic acid. Buy natural spring water, preferably, bottled at the source.

"Some people using chlorinated water fill gallon jugs and let them sit on the counter for 24 hours without a lid. The chlorine will dissipate, but the harmful resonance signature remains. Ozone is safer. It's also a better disinfectant. Some purveyors of bottled water simply filter out the chlorine from conventionally treated water. That's why spring water is superior to ordinary bottled water.

"Some cities also add fluoride to their water. It is even more lethal than chlorine and should be strictly avoided. Many years ago ranchers began spiking livestock water with fluoride to keep their herds docile. Today it is added to municipal drinking water with the same hidden intent. Many of the new anti-depressant drugs, including Prozac, are fluoride-based. Don't even use fluoride toothpaste, or let your hygienist give you a fluoride treatment. Plenty of information can be found on the Internet on the dangers of both chlorine and fluoride, but you must also use your imagination to establish self-knowledge."

M: "What about distilled water?"

JR: "All contaminants are removed in the distillation process, but the pH is around 6.9. It draws from its surroundings. This includes energy. When low-energy distilled water is introduced into a high-energy body, it will drain life-force from the system. In addition, pure distilled water at 10 degrees centigrade is 96% pentagonally structured. Hexagonally [six-sided] structured water is healthier to drink.[9]

"The pH scale runs from 0–14, with 7 being neutral. Water breaks down into two ions, the hydrogen ion (H+), and the hydroxyl ion (OH-). The pH scale actually measures the 'hydrogen ion concentration.' Any substance having more oxygen, in the form of hydroxyl ions, is considered basic, or alkaline. These substances have a pH designation above 7. Acids have more hydrogen ions, and occupy the region below 7. Distilled water falls into this category. Low pH water will deteriorate the inside lining of iron distribution pipes. For this reason, municipal agencies treat their water with soda ash, lime, or sodium hydroxide to boost the pH.

"For robust health, the hydrogen and oxygen in our bodies must be balanced; hence the healing success of hydrogen peroxide (H_2O_2).[10] The typical 'American diet' of fast foods and soft drinks overloads the body with acid and promotes solidification and weight gain. Besides low energy, imbalances of hydrogen and oxygen can lead to more severe health problems.

"Since the oxygen in our atmosphere has been reduced through deforestation and pollution, oxygen is at a premium. Our bodies have plenty of fuel, but insufficient oxygen to burn it cleanly.[11] Air bubbles trapped in fossilized amber were found to contain oxygen levels of 38%. Yet today, the oxygen content of our air is around 19% to 21%—about half. This suggests that the human body was designed to operate at twice the oxygen level than we now enjoy. Oxygen has been measured at a shocking 12% to 15% in large cities. Levels below 7% cannot support life.[12]

"In short, the pH of the blood must stay within a narrow margin of 7.3 to 7.45. This is called *homeostasis*. Straying from this delicate range results in death. Because of our low pH, acidic (hydrogen) diet consisting of meat, pop, and artificial foods, our blood pH rides on the low end of its limits. This makes it impossible for the body to assimilate large amounts of additional acid. It must solidify the acid and file it away until the blood pH can be raised; hence the extra pounds. Popular storage places for this acid waste are hips, waists, and around vital organs. This blocks the flow of water, light, and oxygen to cells. This is why disease is generally associated with a highly acidic (low pH), anaerobic (low oxygen) system.

"Dr. Keiichi Morishita substantiates this fact in *The Hidden Truth of Cancer.* He states that if the blood develops a more acidic condition, then these excess acidic wastes have to be deposited somewhere in the body. If this unhealthy process continues year after year, these areas steadily increase in acidity, and cells begin to die.[13]

"Water with pH levels above 7.45 will raise the pH level of the blood. Acids and bases neutralize each other and form water and salts. Raising the body pH with alkaline foods and high pH water can neutralize acid waste. This can result in better health and weight loss. Some natural spring waters have pH values above 8. The pH of water can also be adjusted upward to around 10 through electrolysis.[14]

"The aged citizens of Hunza, who live disease-free to upwards of one hundred years—some claim to be over 150 years old—drink water with a high pH.[15] This undoubtedly contributes to their above average health and extended lifespan. Of course they don't have a McDonald's on every corner, either. By contrast, many young people in this country think nothing of consuming several super-sized soft drinks each day.[16]

"Notice that the chemical formulas for acids generally start with an 'H,' like sulfuric acid: H_2SO_4. The fizz in pop comes from carbon dioxide. The CO_2 combines with water to form carbonic acid (H_2CO_3). This is why the pH of cola is so low, around 2.1! Soft drink consumers don't understand that diet soda is almost as fattening as regular pop because of the low pH. They both get stored away in the same manner. It is this low pH, not the calories, that does the greatest damage to our figure.[17]

"While we're on the subject of diet sodas, you should also know that 'aspartame,' the artificial sweetener found in these drinks, is a deadly toxin. When the temperature of aspartame exceeds 86 degrees Fahrenheit, the wood alcohol in the sweetener converts first to formaldehyde, and then to formic acid, the chemical fire ants use to paralyze their prey. The result is metabolic acidosis.[18]

"Metabolic acidosis mimics MS and a number of other central nervous system disorders. MS is not a death sentence, but methanol toxicity is. Aspartame use—three to four 12-ounce cans of diet pop per day— can result in Fibromyalgia symptoms, spasms, slurred speech, blurred vision, numbness in legs, seizures, cramps, vertigo, dizziness, tinnitus, depression, anxiety attacks, and memory loss. Aspartame, marketed as NutraSweet, Equal, Spoonful, etc., is now in over 5,000 products. If you see the words 'sugar free' or 'light' on the label, avoid it like the plague.[19]

"But back to the subject of water... not only do we fail to drink enough, we drink it at the wrong time. We should drink water throughout the day rather than with meals. One pattern would be a 12-ounce glass first thing in the morning, 20 ounces mid-morning, 20 ounces mid-afternoon, and another 12 ounces prior to retiring. It should not interfere with our meals. A rule of thumb for drinking water is one-half hour before mealtime and three hours after.

"Aquarius is known as the *Water-Bearer*. When his gift to the New Age is fully understood and appreciated, water will rightly take its place as the 'elixir of the gods.'

"The Age of Aquarius will be known as the 'Age of Water.' We will look to 'designer waters,' water with different molecular shapes and clusters, spin rotations, surface tensions, pH qualities, etc., to facilitate the cleanup of the environment and to revitalize the human body. The relationship between the perfect, six-sided molecular cluster—structured water—and the human cell will take center stage in the coming cycle. Musical imprints and vital energy will further enhance these already potent designer waters. The therapeutic value of hydrotherapy and healing spas will also be rediscovered. They will become an integral part of every community.

"As our self-knowledge deepens, we will begin to see the causal relationship between health and past actions. In time, we may discover that much of the dying action in the physical body is a reflection of unbalanced thoughts in the Seedbed tied directly to the killing of animals. This imbalance is reflected on the physical level in the pH scale.

"Metaphysically speaking, where love is lacking, the pH will be lower. On the inner planes, oxygen is directly related to the resonance of love. On the other hand, hydrogen is associated with solidifying and grounding. The positive aspect of hydrogen is gratitude. Water imbued with both love and gratitude will be most beneficial.

"The dying action in the human body manifests in a variety of diseases and addictions that destroy our health, including alcoholism, cancer, and AIDS. For those presently dealing with life-threatening conditions, the taking of life in the animal kingdom should be part of the understanding section of the Golden Formula." [See the Golden Formula template, p. 91.]

The fire was burning low. Goldie had inched closer and closer to the hearth in an attempt to capture the last breath of heat. The Chief sensed that it was time to stretch and fetch more wood.

JR: "One more thing on the subject of health in the coming age. Since the Harmonic Convergence on August 17th [1987], the cells in our bodies have been undergoing a change, an upgrade, so to speak. They will continue to be upgraded as we enter the new cycle, so we can deal with the high-intensity light of the Photon Belt and utilize the planet's new morphogenic codes. Water can facilitate this process.

"Our present flesh and blood cells are transforming into crystalline, fiber optic cells. This will eventually result in the transfiguration of man into a cosmic light-being! He will then resonate with the higher fourth-dimensional frequency, and his lifespan will stretch out before him like moonbeams upon the ocean."

*   *   *

I have no doubt that water is the gold of tomorrow, and if it has value someone will try to regulate it, tax it, or hoard it. So enjoy it while you can. In my humble opinion it is worth more than gold, for all the gold in the world cannot buy good health.

Many years after the Chief's discussion on water, I found out for myself how dehydration can wreak havoc on the body. At that time I was only drinking about 12 ounces a day, far less than the Chief had advised. In my case, dehydration caused severe blood sugar problems. The life-threatening experience taught me two very important lessons, however. I learned that many doctors know little about water, and I learned what the Chief had meant by "establishing self-knowledge."

After struggling with low energy and an occasional blackout, I turned to a naturopathic doctor for assistance. A blood test revealed a blood sugar level of around 40. Blood sugar levels below this point can be fatal. A change in diet was recommended to complement an inner cleansing program. But after contemplating on my problem using the Golden Formula, I experienced a strange sequence of synchronous events that warned of complications, and led to my discovery of the true cause of my condition.

Since I was the first to arrive at work in the morning at the water treatment plant where I was employed at the time, I generally made the coffee. One morning my coworkers complained. The coffee was worse than usual. This particular morning it tasted like soap. Upon investigation, we discovered that someone had washed the coffee pot the night before, but had failed to rinse it out thoroughly. A thin film of soap remained. This was November.

The following month I celebrated Christmas with my brother's family. As we toasted the holiday season with sparkling cider, his wife wrinkled up her nose. Even before she spoke, I guessed the problem. Someone had failed to rinse the champagne glass after washing it. A pattern was developing. My Higher Self was attempting to answer my question about health.

As the New Year approached, I did something very much out of character. I drew a steaming hot bubble bath. Scooping up a handful of bubbles to test the fragrance, I inadvertently inhaled a large soap bubble. The strong soapy taste was nauseating. As I consumed my second twelve-ounce glass of cold water, the answer flashed into my mind.

Water—large amounts of water! That was what my body craved. The toxins I was dislodging with my inner cleansing program were not being flushed from my system.

My inner guidance also led me to a local bookstore. While browsing through their section on health, I came across a book written by an Iranian doctor who had been wrongly imprisoned by his government. While in prison, he had been given permission to treat his fellow inmates. There was only one catch. He could use no medication, only water. But miracle of miracles, he achieved great success in treating even the most debilitating diseases. His incarceration had come with a silver lining.

Dr. Batmanghelidj's work has largely been ignored, even ridiculed, by the pharmaceutical industry, but his book, *Your Body's Many Cries for Water*, has helped many open-minded doctors and countless people like myself who have suffered from chronic dehydration. His advice: "You are not sick, you are thirsty! Don't treat thirst with medications!"[20]

*　　　　　*　　　　　*

Q. What can I do to achieve better health in my life?

A. ... add more water to the system, systematically taken that the acid in the system may be dissolved.

– Edgar Cayce, 1925[21]

ENHANCED SPRING WATER

When I'm asked what kind of water is best, I defer to the Chief: "We should drink the highest-quality water we can find." If we contemplate on water—put it in a mental picture using the imagination—we will be led to the right one for us.

In general, however, natural spring waters from deep aquifers yield the highest purity with slightly elevated pH values. They also taste great. The purveyors of these waters will tell you the pH and answer pertinent questions. I prefer brands bottled at the source, with no additional treatment. (Ozonation is an acceptable method of disinfection.)

I also look for small, six-sided molecular clusters (snowflakes) that radiate light and channel electromagnetic energy and information. Dr. Masaru Emoto, who took the world's first pictures of frozen water crystals, examined water from around the world and catalogued his findings in *Messages from Water*.[22] His pictures also show how sound, music, energy, and even the human voice, leave signature imprints on water, both harmonious and discordant.

Spring water can be enhanced through a variety of methods to better accommodate our transition to the Photon Belt. For FAQ's and additional information about enhanced spring water, including how to make Flower of Life Supercrystals™ and Therapeutic Gemstone Water, see the following website: www.SusanCreek.com.[23]

PART III

CROSSING THE GOLDEN THRESHOLD

CHILDREN OF THE BUTTERFLY PARADIGM

The forecast was calling for a white Christmas. When I followed the Chief out to the carport for more wood around seven p.m., I was thrilled to discover a light dusting of snow on the roof of my car. I loved this time of the year—the colorful lights, the decorations, the feeling of joy permeating the atmosphere. The Christmas I'd celebrated in Honolulu was perhaps my happiest. But traditionally, December meant skiing with friends and visiting family in Oregon. Spending time with the Chief was an added blessing.

Once inside the cabin I asked the Chief how we should prepare for the shift in frequency that would lift humanity beyond the third dimension. He stepped over Goldie and threw a large fir log on the fire before answering. Sparks erupted in a violent plume, as the heavy log crashed through the slumbering coals.

The Chief stirred the fire absentmindedly as he spoke. "The Shift of the Ages... isn't it amazing? We are poised on the threshold of the most exciting event in human history, yet only a small number of people know anything about it." A look of disbelief accompanied a shake of his head. As I reflected on the musings of my teacher, I had to remind myself that this great transmutation was happening in our very midst; it was not some vague prediction from an uncertain future.

Muffled sounds from the front porch brought Goldie clumsily to her feet. A cheerful woman in her mid-fifties and her bright-eyed grandson peered timidly through the opening door. They'd brought a gift for the Chief, a plate of fudge. By the conversation, I surmised that the woman was a fellow gardener who lived somewhere along Little River.

The Chief bent down on one knee and asked the boy what he thought about the unexpected snowfall. He smiled broadly, showing a fencerow of baby teeth before retreating behind his grandmother. After sharing some cider and chitchat about garden pests and caterpillars, the woman left with her grandson in tow. The Chief offered me a piece of fudge and continued.

"In a way, the transformation of caterpillars into butterflies parallels our transcendence of the physical plane. The caterpillar has never been a butterfly before, and we've never been through a shift of this magnitude." He chuckled. "Both of us are venturing into uncharted territory.

"Let's explore this metaphor a bit further. If our tiny friend had the mental capacity to evaluate the changes before him, perhaps he'd set some goals, or perhaps plan out a timetable. And why not try some visualization? In his imagination he might see himself with long, powerful legs, jumping over small twigs and fallen limbs that he now must climb over. He might work on his upper body strength to better scale the mountainous compost heap by the garden. If that's what butterflies do? Our ambitious caterpillar might share his aspirations of jumping and climbing with his friends. He might even ask their take on the coming metamorphosis. Surely they would know about this life-changing event! Do you see the problem?

"Anything the caterpillar does is solely within the framework of becoming 'a better caterpillar.' Nothing exists in his current paradigm to prepare him for rebirth as a butterfly. The idea of flight would never cross his mind. So how in the world does this great transformation take place, you might ask? *It just happens!*" I gave a nod of approval.

"As we discussed earlier, preparation for changes of any kind should begin with contemplation. If not, we will react with the same old programming. When it's our time to fly, we don't want rusty chains holding us to the ground. Moreover, once we have established self-knowledge, we will begin to relax. Our intuition can then guide us moment by moment. As we gain a greater understanding of Earth's ascension process, we will come to trust what is happening behind the scenes.

"On August 17th [1987] the world was first touched by the Dragon's Breath. This monumental event initiated at least two important processes that have been lifting the frequency of the Earth and its people. These are (1) an update of the morphogenic field, or code, from which we will draw our ideas for the next cycle; in other words, the new paradigm, and (2) an acceleration of the balancing of the Global Seedbed, or world karma. We touched on the latter point when we discussed the individual Seedbed, so let's focus on the code.

"While the morphogenic field of the sun is being upgraded, our personal codes encrypted on the DNA are changing, as well. This rate of change will vary from individual to individual, depending on our mean energy floating point. From your eighth grade science primer you may recall that DNA consists of a single double-helix coiled in a spiral. Since the Harmonic Convergence, however, the unthinkable is happening. Additional strands of DNA have been forming!" [News of this change in the DNA has been withheld from the public under the pretense that it would frighten the population. Perhaps they feel this mutation would conjure up images of the Incredible Hulk.]

M: "Are baby boomers and their parents growing new strands, as well?"

JR: "To one degree or another, everything on Earth is changing at the DNA level. Baby boomers came in with less baggage than either their parents or grandparents, so their shift to the new frequency will go much smoother. The impetus for awakening actually comes from the Higher Self of each individual. For this reason, the transition will not be en masse as some New Age philosophies claim.

"Changes to the physical body are inevitable as new DNA strands are formed. The original blueprint calls for 12. We may find that we're tired a lot, for example, as the body detoxifies and releases trapped emotional energy to accommodate the higher frequency. As we talked about earlier, lower-frequency emotions will rise to the surface and be passed off. Anything that gives us physical discomfort, mental anguish, or emotional pain must go."

Goldie shot the Chief an agitated look as she passed by his chair en route to the kitchen. It was her way of telling him that her dinner was late. While the Chief was occupied, I checked out the weather from the back porch. The snow was still falling.

[Two experiences, both from the summer of 2001, proved helpful to me in clarifying the relationship between the aforementioned "physical discomfort" and our transition to the Photon Belt. At the risk of breaking the flow of our discussion, I have included them here.

In August of that year I met a fascinating individual, a Persian master, at a lecture held at a nearby hall. We talked at length about Earth's transition to multi-dimensionality. During our three-hour conversation, she verified much of the data I had gathered from the Chief. The intensity of her magnetic field, however, triggered an inner cleansing within my physical body.

For several days after the encounter I experienced a raging fever. Wave after wave of energy washed through my body in the form of chills. Surprisingly, my consciousness remained bright during the week-long cleansing. I realized that I was experiencing an upgrade, and let the cleansing run its course without interference.

My "coughing experience" wasn't as pleasant. That same summer I came down with an annoying cough that lingered on. When I showed no sign of improvement, I was urged by friends and coworkers to "take something for it." I trusted my intuition and kept coughing.

One night I discovered the reason for my affliction. Unable to sleep, I paced back and forth across my tiny living room, coughing uncontrollably. Following an inner nudge, I sent my consciousness deeper and deeper into the pain. A startling revelation began to unfold. With each trip across the floor a different personality from my past appeared before my spiritual vision.

I was the captain of a ship, flung overboard to my death by a mutinous crew. I was an elderly English gentleman, whose throat had been slit in a dark London alley; and a man of unknown origin, hanged on the gallows in an ancient square. I was the mother of a baby who lay dying in my arms... and an enemy of the state, sent to the guillotine in the French revolution.

All in all, perhaps eight or nine scenes flashed by in rapid succession. Through each violent cough echoed words I'd choked back, words pregnant with emotion—terror, rage, and unspeakable sorrow. I left nothing unexpressed; I screamed, cursed, apologized, and wept.

Finally I returned to bed, exhausted from the ordeal, but feeling better having released the pain. My throat chakra had been clogged all my life. Now I understood why.]

After letting Goldie out to take care of her nightly business, the Chief returned from the kitchen with a pitcher of water and a small plate of fudge. After refilling my glass, he continued with our topic of change.

"An interesting phenomenon is taking place in many parts of the world. Children are being born with multiple strands of DNA. Scientists say they have special abilities. But it's more than that. They carry the new morphogenic codes! I think of them as *Butterfly Children.*

"Many of these new arrivals have associations with the ancient Land of MU, as well as the Pleiadian and Sirian systems. Some know who they've been; a few know who they are. They come both as teachers and as artists to usher in a new renaissance where technology will no longer take the forefront. Some believe them to be the progenitors of a new root-race.

"They exemplify the new paradigm. These children are unorthodox by present standards; they don't fit into the old way of thinking, nor do they want to. They may not know at this point why the world doesn't feel right. They simply know it must change.

"By observing these children we can get some idea of what life will hold for us in the forthcoming cycle. They exhibit common traits, no matter where in the world they've been born. They are intuitive, for instance, even psychic, having the ability to send messages over long distances telepathically. Some can move matter with their minds; some can manifest objects. There have been documented cases where empty water glasses have been filled by direct manifestation."

[A book called *The Indigo Children,* written by Lee Carroll and Jan Tober, introduced these children to the world in 1999. Indigo relates to the predominant color emanating from their auric field, a color sometimes associated with the Aquarian Age. To James Twyman, author of *Emissary of Love,* they are "Psychic Children." In *Notes from the Cosmos,* Gordon Michael Scallion calls them "Children of the Blue Ray." An intriguing picture of a butterfly encased in a chrysalis heads Scallion's chapter by the same name. It is also interesting to note that Butterfly Children are often drawn to water, be it a lake, river, or ocean.]

JR: "Besides their psychic abilities, these children have come in with many of the understandings we still struggle with. Therefore, their main focus isn't learning, it is teaching. As they enter our school system, they will challenge the distortions of truth presented to them as facts. Either that, or they will simply look out the window at the clouds.

"Not all children born since the Harmonic Convergence have psychic abilities or multiple strands of DNA, but 90% of them arrive with the new vibration. While they, too, have karma to balance, they possess high self-esteem, vivid imaginations, and great determination. They believe in self-authority. When unnecessarily controlled, which is just about anytime in their opinion, they rebel or act out. They do this not out of insolence, but because control feels painful to them. They are often misunderstood, labeled as problem children, and then drugged. But even so, they know they are royalty. They wait with impatience for the changing of the guard.

"Once the present cycle steeped in fear and control has ended, Earth will experience a freedom never before imagined. Those born under the influence of the Dragon's Breath will not come fully alive or feel at home until we are completely immersed in the new paradigm.

"Many of the Butterfly Children have the ability to communicate with animals and plants. A large number are vegetarians, or will be. They also understand why various species of animals have chosen to leave the planet at this time."

I'd recently heard from a questionable source that most of the cows would be leaving the planet. It conjured up images of *Far Side* cartoons. I envisioned a herd of cows standing upright on a train platform, holding their bags. The Chief smiled politely at my feeble attempts at humorous captions. To me, the idea that nearly every cow would be leaving the Earth seemed too preposterous to be anything but a joke. But this was before staggering numbers of cattle were slaughtered during the Mad Cow fiasco. And who could forget the dinosaurs! The Chief had some insights into the matter.

JR: "Much misunderstanding surrounds the nature of our friends, the animals. Propaganda aimed at the perpetuation of violence and fear has done them much harm. This dates back to the advent of the Belief System, nearly 400,000 years ago." The Chief smiled. "I can't speak to the travel plans of cows, but I'm happy to say that things are changing.

"Since the lowest-vibration negativity cannot pass through the dimensional threshold, it must be cleared from our Seedbed. But what about the negativity of animals? Like humans, they too can be selfish, proud, stubborn, fearful, belligerent, angry, cowardly, and so forth."

My thoughts drifted back to a remarkably accurate spitting llama I'd encountered at a petting zoo... and a childhood pet, a goat named Dumbo, who could be surly, as well. Whenever friends came to visit, Dumbo would ram them from behind when their backs were turned. Come to think about it, all my pets had been temperamental, at best.

JR: "When man began creating more karma than he could balance in a single lifetime, it posed an unexpected problem—what to do with his negativity while he retired to the astral plane between lives? His Seedbed could not go with him.

"It was at this point in time that the animals stepped up to assist the hierarchy. A number of species volunteered to carry a portion of man's Seedbed in his absence from Earth. This would continue until the Seedbed had been cleared or until the dimensional shift, whichever came first. Well, finally, with the ending of the Piscean Age, their service in this manner will no longer be necessary.

"The behavior of animals will dramatically improve after the shift, as will their relationship with man.

Even so, certain species have asked to be lifted off the planet."

M: I scratched my head. "So, many of the endangered species are simply wrapping up their contracts here?"

JR: "That's a good way of looking at it. But this doesn't mean we should further pollute their habitat, or be indifferent to their plight. Animals deserve our love and respect, as well as our gratitude. We must rely on our intuition to tell us what to do."

This subject triggered several emotions: sadness, anger, guilt, and confusion. It was a tip-off that I harbored conflicting thought patterns in my Seedbed relating to the treatment of animals. The Chief had once mentioned that a vegetarian diet was most conducive to the shift. I made a mental note to run this issue through the Golden Formula. My hand reached for a piece of fudge, perhaps to temporarily quell this inner conflict, as the Chief continued.

JR: "In 1845 Thoreau reflected in his book, *Walden,* that 'man is rich in proportion to the number of things he can afford to leave alone.'[1] It's a powerful observation, even today. As compassionate people, we instinctively rush to change things we find disturbing. But is it always advisable? Are there situations best left alone? It's an interesting question to ponder.

"For example, one morning I rescued an earthworm from the middle of a parking lot after a summer rainstorm. Ever so carefully I placed him on a lush patch of green grass out of harms way. What a kind gesture, I thought. But when I retired that evening, other possibilities came to mind.

"What if the tiny creature had struggled throughout the stormy night to reach the place of his destiny, the middle of the asphalt jungle? What if later that morning the future 'mrs. worm' had also arrived at that spot, only to find the parking lot empty? Had I done the worm a favor by sweeping him off to safety? Had my own fears and judgments influenced my decision to interfere in his life? No doubt.

"While it is human nature to want things to be perfect, from a cosmic point of view perfection lacks excitement. To a filmmaker, a perfect movie is not someone sitting by a lake sipping lemonade in scene after scene. It is a movie that stirs the emotions, one with problems and crises. That's why our dramas make for interesting movies. But drama after drama soon becomes tedious. We crave variety. We yearn for comedies, adventures, romances, even horror films. We desperately need our antagonists and villains. What's the name of that movie about the shark?"

M: "Jaws?"

JR: "That's it. Can you imagine reading a review in the paper that goes something like this: 'It would have been the perfect movie...if only the writer had left out the shark.'" It was a good point. But I confided to the Chief that sipping lemonade by the lake didn't sound half-bad right now.

M: "Is there a predominant theme for the Aquarian Age?"

JR: "The Golden Age of Aquarius will be governed by the 7th Cosmic Ray.[2] Therefore, the theme for the next two thousand years will be *Unity and Order*. The Internet is a good example of this trend toward unification. Once humanity has been united, the "spiritual Internet" will be found, the Golden Thread. This will happen sometime in the coming cycle.

"The higher aspect of Unity encompasses brotherhood and cooperation. So, in other words, we'll have plenty of lemonade. But first we may see the lower aspect of the ray take the forefront; hence the push for a one-world government motivated by greed, corruption, and totalitarian control (lemons). With the dimensional shift low on the horizon, however, the period of negativity will be short-lived.

"The Kal Power is never allowed to completely take over. If things get too bad, look for Divine Intervention. Miracles can and do happen.

"With foreknowledge of the coming changes, we can relax and appreciate the final act in the Piscean Age play for what it is. We can inform others about the new paradigm and the renaissance to come. Many will not listen. They will be too caught up in the 'last days scenario' and the scripted misinformation world leaders will be espousing.

"Most importantly, as we approach 2012 we can move ahead with our primary responsibility—the cleaning out of our Seedbed. This will assure us safe passage through the time of purification as predicted by many Native American peoples. We can then catch the golden wave of multi-dimensional light to our next stop on the pathway home."

*　　　　　*　　　　　*

There is a tide in the affairs of men,
which, taken at the flood
leads on to fortune;
omitted, all the voyage of their life
is bound in shallows and in miseries.

– William Shakespeare
Julius Caesar, IV, iii[3]

2012 AND THE BLUE STAR PROPHECY

Aside from the Chief, I've heard only a small number of people mention the importance of 2012, even in passing. Information on the Photon Belt is an even greater scarcity. Most of those I've told about the coming changes have been less than enthusiastic—no big surprise. Some have even rolled their eyes. Who knows, had I not listened to the Chief's words with my own ears, I might have done the same. I have to admit, compared to *Oprah* or *Sportscenter* it is pretty far out stuff.

But I have little doubt that the Chief was right about 2012 and the Photon Belt, even Earth's multidimensional future. I know for sure that the Golden Formula and the Chief's principle of non-resistance are rooted in truth. I've also had visions of an Earth bathed in gold, an Earth barely recognizable because it shimmers with light. Even so, I used to wake up in the middle of the night and lie awake agonizing about the accuracy of the Chief's information. It would also bother me when skeptics would raise the question, "What if the Chief was wrong?"

I've had a number of years to think about this, and I would now address their challenge as follows: "If there are indeed a hundred billion stars in the Milky Way as astronomers claim, and a hundred billion galaxies like our own, in the grand scheme of things does it really matter whether the Chief was right or wrong?"

Personally, I believe that 2012 marks the birth of a new Golden Age. I'm also intrigued by three things: 1) that Divine Intervention could alter the timetable of events, 2) that a massive shift in consciousness could catapult us into the Golden Age prior to 2012, and 3) that a split in reality could occur when we enter the Photon Belt. (See "The Dividing of the Way," later in this chapter.) But it really doesn't matter what I believe... or even what the Chief believed.

Many people will dismiss the material presented here anyway, no matter how insightful. It will be at odds with what they've been taught; in other words, it will be contrary to the contents of their Belief System. This is why any outside information should be viewed simply as seed material for contemplation. As the Chief stressed so often, it is entirely up to us to establish our own self-knowledge. Verification is solely our responsibility. Had I not believed this myself I would never have written this book. However, for the benefit of others who may need further inspiration and seed material for contemplation, I've included some additional information on 2012 and the Photon Belt.

In *Beyond Prophecies and Predictions,* Moira Timms describes planetary initiation as "a time when spiritual consciousness aligns with the dynamics of the cosmos: when the people of the Earth, the Earth itself, and the solar system experience a shift—an awesome, majestic, eschatological heave into the fourth dimension. What will be available to us by the year 2012

A.D. will be so rich and deep it is hard for us to conceptualize it."[1]

Sun Bear, the late medicine chief of the Bear Tribe Medicine Society, echoed Timms' sentiment. "By the year 2012," he stated, "it's going to get very, very interesting to watch...I see major changes coming."[2] In preparing for the shift, Sun Bear advised working on the higher consciousness and self-responsibility, as did John Redstone.

Millie Moore, one of Paul Twitchell's first students, also spoke of planetary initiation on several occasions. In 1999 she addressed the physical changes associated with this transformation:

> All cycles of the last 100,000 years are aligning at once. In a short time we will not just be in three dimensions. The planet is going through initiation...We are changing physically because we are learning to handle our multi-dimensional beingness, we are moving into the fourth dimension. Our bodies are being transmuted into this higher rate of vibration.[3]

Cosmic initiation is a fascinating subject; however, it is also vast and complicated, requiring a broad base of spiritual knowledge to fully understand and appreciate it. This is evident when you read Alice Bailey's works. Therefore, rather than offer a cursory view and risk confusion, I've decided to focus mainly on 2012 and the Photon Belt.

The year 2012 was an important date to both the Mayans and the Aztecs. It is also prominent in the Incan, Tibetan, and Native American cultures. To the Lakota, Cherokee, and Hopi, this time in history is the close of a grand cycle leading to the birth of a new world.[4] It is said that the trigrams of the I-Ching also point to an end date of 2012.[5] Information about 2012 has also come from surprising sources.

According to Sean David Morton, scientists at the Rand Corporation discovered that a polar shift would occur in the year 2012. They classified their astonishing research, believing that the public should be shielded from such catastrophic information. Eventually the secret leaked out, however, and *Time Magazine* even featured their findings on a cover. When the American people showed little interest in the story, the Rand Corporation declassified their files![6]

End of the Mayan Calendar

Five thousand years ago the mysterious Maya, the architects of massive temples and celestial observatories in the Yucatan peninsula, predicted that this world would end on December 21, 2012 A.D. It should be noted, however, that to many ancient cultures, including the Aztec and Hopi, the term "world" meant "a cycle of time." On the heels of one world's demise another would begin.

The Mayan calendar is considered by scholars to be one of the oldest and most sophisticated systems of timekeeping known to mankind. Until the advent of our atomic clocks, based on the vibrations of the cesium atom, the Mayan calendar rivaled the accuracy of any records of time known before the twentieth century. Descendants of the Maya to this day ascertain the correct date through a system that, according to experts, has "not slipped one day in over twenty-five centuries!"[7]

Key to the Mayan timekeepers was a 260-day count called the *tzolkin,* or "Sacred Calendar," based on the cycle of the Pleiades.[8] Common among other Mesoamerican traditions, as well, the *tzolkin* is created as the interface between twenty named days and a counter based on the number thirteen. The Maya, however, carried their timekeeping a step further. Intermeshed with a 365-day count called the "Vague Year," the two cycles of time progressed like the cogs of two wheels until the rare moment when one day on the Sacred Calendar matched the same day of the Vague Year. That day marked the end of a fifty-two-year cycle.[9]

The 26,000-year-long Mayan Great Calendar also mirrors the Grand Precession of the Equinoxes. Furthermore, both the Maya and Aztecs recognize an even longer cycle 104,000 years in duration. This cycle consists of four Great Cycles of 26,000 years each. 2,160 of these 104,000-year cycles amount to 225-million-years. This is the time it takes for our solar system to complete one Galactic Orbit. Along with the 2,160-year Piscean age, all three of these extended cycles are scheduled to end in 2012.[10]

According to Mayan chronology, the cycle we're now in started on August 12, 3114 B.C., and will end on the winter solstice in 2012.[11] This event has been anticipated by the Mayans for over five thousand years.[12]

August 17, 1987, Birth of the Aztec Sixth Sun

The Aztec calendar tracks great cycles of time as "Suns," rather than the Mayan "worlds." According to their calendar we are living in the closing days of the Fifth Sun. Their history tells of the First Sun, called *Nahui Ocelotl*. It was a time when giants lived within the Earth. This ancient race devoured all which the labor of men produced until it became impossible to feed them. This period ended when the animal kingdom overcame the human kingdom.

During the Second Sun, *Nahui Ehecatl*, human beings began cultivating the Earth and crossbreeding plants. This period ended when a great wind swept across the face of the Earth, clearing everything in its path.

Great temples and cities were constructed during the Third Sun, *Nahui Quiauhuitl*. Tremendous openings in the Earth and a "rain of fire" marked the end of this cycle according to the Aztecs. Our geological records indicate that portions of the Earth appeared to have been covered with fire. The ending of the Fourth Sun has been confirmed geologically, as well. This event, the Great Flood, has been passed down by oral and written tradition by many peoples throughout the world.

On August 17, 1987, the Fifth Sun cycle of the Aztecs came to a close. The Harmonic Convergence, the mid-point of the 50-year, Time/Space Overlap Zone between the Piscean Age and the Age of Aquarius, marked the birth of the Sixth Sun of the ancient Aztecs.[13]

The Tibetan "Wheel of Time"

The Tibetan calendar is called the *Kalachakra*, or "Wheel of Time." It contains a prophecy that 860 years after its introduction into Tibet, which happened in 1127, the conditions would be fulfilled for a twenty-five year period that would culminate in the appearance of the sacred Tibetan spiritual city known as Shamballa —860 years after 1127 is 1987. Twenty-five years after that is 2012![14]

Presently the spiritual city is reported to exist in the supra-physical regions slightly beyond our current range of perception. The Tibetan prophecy would indicate that Earth is indeed on the verge of a great transformation. When the vibrations of the planet have been sufficiently raised, not only will we be able to visit Shamballa, but also many other spiritual cities that were lifted into the etheric realms. Had the spiritual hierarchy not done this, many or all would have met with the same fate as those monasteries overrun by Chinese invaders in the 1950's.

The Hopi "Blue Star Prophecy"

Similar to the traditions of the Maya and Aztecs, the Hopi of the American Southwest believe that previous periods of human experience have ended in destruction, the most recent being the Great Flood. They also believe that we are presently living in one such transition period, "a time of purification."

The Hopi have disclosed "three prophetic signs" denoting a timetable for the Great Shift. The first sign was the appearance of the moon "on the Earth as well as the heavens." The fulfillment of this portion of the prophecy remained a total mystery until 1993, when lunar images began to appear as crop circles in the grain fields of the English countryside. The unmistakable images of the crescent moon were interpreted by Hopi elders to be the fulfillment of the first portion of the prophecy.[15]

The second sign was the appearance of the "Blue Star," a prominent symbol found in many Hopi traditions. According to tradition, the appearance of this Blue Star heralds the beginning of the *Great Purification*. The fulfillment of this portion of the prophecy remains a subject of debate. The appearance of the Blue Star is foretold in a song that was sung at the major ceremony of the Hopi annual cycle in 1914, 1940, and 1961. They expected that the next time the Blue Star ceremony was performed, it would finally appear.[16]

On February 22, 1987, something spectacular happened in the heavens that relates to the Hopi prophecy and roughly coincides with the Harmonic Convergence. A distant star located in the Greater Magellanic Cloud, a sub-galaxy of our Milky Way, exploded in stupendous fashion creating a stir among stargazers on this world. The supernova, a gigantic blue star, shone with a brilliance 200 million times greater than the sun of our system at its peak. It was the brightest supernova to be detected in four centuries, and was immediately heralded as one of the most significant scientific events of the century. The star had actually exploded 170,000 years ago, but it took that long for the wave of electric blue light to reach the shores of our planet.

Some also believe the appearance of the blue star in the heavens fulfilled a prophecy coded in the Great Pyramid of Giza, and was attuned to the re-opening of the long dormant Temple of Inscriptions at Palenque in Mexico.[17]

Gordon-Michael Scallion believes the Hale-Bopp Comet, discovered by two amateur astronomers on July 23, 1995, is the long-awaited Blue Star Messenger, whose arrival signals our next spiritual awakening. Scallion claims this same Blue Star visited Earth eleven thousand six hundred years ago, at the time of the last major shift. It appeared in the heavens to warn of the coming flood and the sinking of Atlantis.[18]

The third and last portion of the Hopi prophecy points to the return of the "sky people." Prominent in the dance, weavings, and sand paintings of the Hopi are curious, humanoid images that often adorn their homes and ceremonial sites. With strange costumes and very otherworldly faces, these representations of Hopi ancestry, the sky people, are called *kachinas*.

The final part of the prophecy states that the great change will occur when the kachinas return from the stars and dance once again in the plazas of their villages on the mesas.[19]

Speaking Wind's Message

According to the late Speaking Wind, a Native American (Pueblo) writer and shaman, the final cleansing of Earth started in June of 1998. Thus began the great tearing away of illusion that will escalate until the fourth world ends on December 22, 2012 A.D., a date taken from "star calendars." At that time, the fifth world—an era of peace and love—will begin.

In June of 1998 people began experiencing waves of depression and anxiety, fulfilling an ancient prophecy. This coincides with the coming on line of the "great weapon" designed to enslave the mind of man through microwave-driven, extra low frequency (ELF) radiation. Cell phone towers, seen popping up everywhere, have the ability to transmit these low frequency waves.[20]

Those who cannot willingly let go of the false reality spun by those presently in control—the illusion that we are limited beings—will have it stripped away. They will suffer depression, memory loss, anxiety, anger, and great inner turmoil. But this will not come as punishment, only to prepare them for the new world that even now can be seen on the distant horizon.[21]

Quetzalcoatl's Prophecy

Over 110 years ago Quetzalcoatl, also known as the "Pale Prophet," imparted a powerful vision to Wavoka, the Paiute elder who called forth the "Ghost Dance." Indigenous people have handed down this prophecy to modern times.

It states that for five full cycles of the Dawn Star (Venus), which amounts to 520 years (5 X 104 years), ending in the year 2012 of the Mayan Calendar, the rule of the *STRANGERS* [emphasis added] would grow into greater and ever greater orgies of death and destruction. The prophecy continues:

> When they have polluted the Earth to such an extent that the number of the Earth becomes 13 then in that moment they shall be no more,[22] the dream shall alter as Hu Nab Ku (Our father in heaven) has a plan a great plan and that cannot be altered...There shall be a shifting, a great shaking and all things shall be touched, even the stones, and in a moment there shall be a newness in a great swelling of light that will fill the heavens and block out even the light of our own sun in its brightness [Dragon's Breath], and the worlds shall split as will the heavens...in a moment. And in that moment you shall be where your heart is *for time as we have known it shall be no more*..[emphasis added].[23]

Days of Light/Days of Darkness

I once asked the Chief about the famous "Three Days of Darkness" prophecy. He believed that it referred to the crossing of the dimensional threshold. If our sun crossed first, he observed, it would not be able to furnish us with light, as it would be in the 4th dimension. If Earth crossed first, we would immediately be thrust into the brilliant light of the Photon Belt.

An article written by the *Star Nation* on prophecy entitled "Truth or Consequences," calls this phenomenon "Days of Light and/or Days of Darkness." It will last approximately 110 hours as we now measure time (four and a half days).[24] While the time frame differs, their explanation mirrors that of the Chief.

The Dividing of the Way

In an article outlining the effects of entering the Photon Belt, Dr. Noel Huntley postulates 3 to 5 days of darkness if our sun crosses the Golden Threshold first. His website, "Duality and Beyond," explores parallel universes, star gates, ascension, and a splitting of reality.

He claims that confirmation of the Photon Band's existence came from astronomers in 1961 through satellite instrumentation. In the early 1980's a radio announcement in the U.S. stated that our solar system was going to collide with an "electromagnetic cloud" in the not too distant future. Follow-up data was suppressed. Dr. Huntley goes on to say that our solar system skimmed the belt for a few days in 1987. Earth is not expected to fully enter until the year 2012. At that time we will experience the full-blown effects.

Photon energy is the result of the collision of electrons and positrons. Their mass is converted into radiation—photons. After 2012, those presently in control will be unable to suppress this new source of free energy. Healing will begin on a personal level, as well as on a planetary scale.

This cosmic encounter will result in the uprooting of deep-seated psychological, emotional, and physical diseases. Old patterns will rise to the surface, and will be passed off. DNA will be upgraded by these new, powerful frequencies. Matter will also be affected by intense photon activity. All objects will appear to fluoresce. Dr. Huntley asserts that this great transformation is the much-heralded "ascension," or "rapture."

According to Dr. Huntley, there will be a dividing of the way, a splitting of reality. After entering the Photon Belt, there will be a 3rd density Earth and a more evolved 4th density Earth. This split will not be perceived physically. The "new Earth" is apparently unoccupied, except for a few animals that have recently left and are waiting for us. Huntley goes on to say that, sadly, some families will be split up. Some individuals will go with the 4th density Earth, while others will stay behind.[25] [Third density Earth may experience the cataclysm that some have predicted.]

A Monument to the End of Time

In the corner of a little known churchyard in the small Basque coastal town of Hendaye, Spain, sits a battered and neglected 300 year-old cross, a monument to the end of time. The faded Greek cross at Hendaye bears Latin inscriptions that are said to reveal the end point of time.[26]

In their book, *A Monument to the End of Time,* Jay Weidner and Vincent Bridges relate that in the 1950's a mysterious author known as Fulcanelli added a new chapter to his twenty year-old book, *Mystery of the Cathedrals.* Weidner and Bridges believe Fulcanelli's impetus for revealing the significance of the cyclic cross at Hendaye at that time was to jump-start the creation of a Golden Age. Fulcanelli believed that this Golden Age, in which humanity rediscovers its spiritual heritage, would occur very soon.[27]

The symbology of the cross reveals a season of destruction from summer solstice to winter solstice over a 20-year period (1992 – 2012), by pointing to its mid-point, the fall equinox of 2002, when the planetary and solar alignments form a right-angled cross between our system's angular momentum and the galactic center.[28] This date coincides with the mid-point of the last Mayan *katun,* calculated from the summer solstice of 1992 to the winter solstice of 2012.[29]

The mid-point of this destructive period foretold by the Hendaye cross falls on September 22, 2002. It is bracketed by celestial events on the solstice, the most prominent of which is the helical rising of the sun and the galactic center on the winter solstice of 2012. As this is the end date of both the Mayan calendar and the Tibetan Kalachakra, its significance becomes even more profound.[30]

Astrologically on December 21, 2012, the sun will rise in perfect alignment with the center of the galaxy on the cusp of Scorpio/Sagittarius while the moon sets on the cusp of Gemini/Taurus. On the summer solstice at the beginning of the twenty-year season of destruction, the moon was conjunct the center of the galaxy and the sun was in opposition. On the winter solstice, the end point, the sun will be conjunct the galactic center, and the moon will be in opposition. Thus the solstice alignments, as revealed on the Hendaye monument, act as book ends to our mid-point of September 22, 2002, defining a 20-year season ending in 2012.[31]

2012 and the 64 "Waves of Time"

Two scientists in the United States, Terrance and Dennis McKenna, believe that the universe is a hologram of 64 waves or time scales, and this is why we have the 64 hexagrams of the I-Ching, 64 keys of the Tree of Life, and the 64 codons of the DNA. Their computer analysis suggests that all 64 of these waves are going to peak together in 2012. This will make the next few years a period of staggering change.

The McKennas say that the speed of change has gone on doubling in a smaller and smaller time frame, manifesting as the leaps in technological development in this century. Projecting forward, they say that this will continue to the transformation year of 2012, when in a period of 384 days, there will be more transformations of consciousness than in all the previous cycles put together! After this there will be a six-day cycle in which events will move even faster, and in the last 135 minutes there will be eighteen further enormous leaps in human consciousness.[32]

Effects of Entering the Photon Belt

In 1995 David Icke included information about the Photon Belt in his book entitled "*...and the truth shall set you free.*" He states that an astronomer, Paul Otto Hesse, claimed to have discovered a belt of immensely powerful energy that he termed the "Photon Belt." Icke goes on to say that it would appear that we have reached the point where this solar system is entering the Photon Belt and its highly charged energy.

The influence of the belt on the Earth began in the early 1960's and affected the thinking of many people, but it was as nothing compared with what will happen over the next 35 years. While it takes approximately 2,000 years to pass through the belt, the biggest impact is when we first enter, and the vibrations and molecular structure of everything has to cope with dramatically changing conditions. This will affect the thinking, behavior, and the physical bodies of all life-forms.

David Icke believes the dramatic weather changes —droughts, floods, melting polar caps, etc.—that have been blamed on global warming (the Greenhouse Effect), are really a diversion from what is actually happening. It is really the result of the Photon Belt and the high frequencies being grounded, the portals opening, and the move from a three-dimensional reality into the fourth and fifth dimensions.[33]

Galactic Photon Bands and the Alcyone Spiral

In *The Pleiadian Agenda,* Barbara Hand Clow describes Photon Bands as seventh-dimensional "donuts of light" that emanate from the vertical axis of the galaxy (Fig. 6). They spin around and around like Ferris Wheels (this author's analogy), penetrating the darkness of the Galactic Night. These Photon Bands contribute to the structure of the galaxy as they rotate around its axis while also serving as information highways.

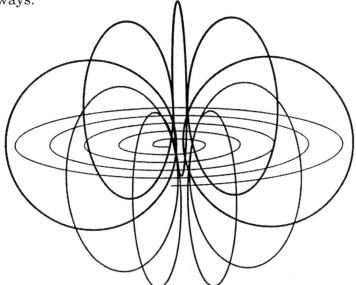

FIGURE 6: GALACTIC PHOTON BANDS[34]

Our Central Sun, Alcyone, constantly resides in one of these Photon Bands. Seven suns, including our own, make up the Alcyone spiral (Fig. 7). Each sun spends approximately 2,000 years of Earth time in this Band of Light. The length of time each sun spends in the Galactic Night, however, is determined by the radius of its orbit around Alcyone.

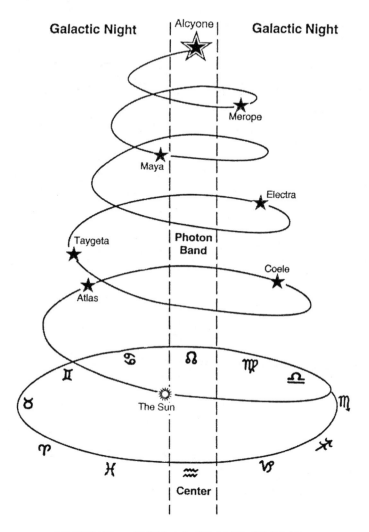

FIGURE 7: THE ALCYONE SPIRAL[35]

Fifth-dimensional light, originating in the Photon Band, spirals out from the Central Sun, connecting each of her seven children in turn: Merope, Maya, Electra, Taygeta, Coele, Atlas, and finally our Sun. Thus, as our legends reveal, Atlas holds the Earth on its shoulders in space.

Due to their close proximity to Alcyone, Merope and Maya spend more time in the Photon Band than they do outside of it. Our solar system, on the other hand, positioned low on the spiral, ventures far into the Galactic Night. We spend approximately 11,000 years in darkness before re-entering the Photon Band for 2,160 years. This is repeated twice in our 26,000-year orbit.[36] Once again we are about to re-enter this magnificent Band of Light.

*   *   *

It's been said that the darkest hour is just before dawn. This holds true when a paradigm ends. Many ancient traditions describe our current transition period as a time of tribulation and purification. Common to these traditions are predictions of great upheavals of both society and nature. Prophecies for our time in history include changing weather patterns, rising temperatures, famines, wars, floods, fires, plagues, droughts, and the general breakdown of all societal infrastructures.

From the popular point of view I see this transition as a good-news/bad-news scenario. The good news is this: An age of prosperity and freedom is on its way. On the other hand, to clear a path for this Golden Age when man will be transformed into a Cosmic Being of Light and Earth ascends to full consciousness, all dysfunctional aspects of our present society must crumble to their foundations—tyrannical governments, self-serving religions, flawed educational institutions, etc. I know, you're probably asking yourself at this moment, "So what's the bad news?"

Of course from a universal point of view there is no news at all, only continuity of the Outbreath and Inbreath of God. Our challenge in the days ahead will be to focus on the positive, and not get caught up in the chaos and uncertainty.

When the changes come, many will cry out, "Where will we be safe? Where should we go? There will be plenty of "authorities" ready to give us their opinion, but will they be trustworthy? Will they be accurate? Will they know our state of consciousness well enough to confidently prescribe a safe haven?

A better question would be, "What should we do to ensure our success and safety in the days ahead?" That one is easy. We should get our own house in order—clean out our Belief System using the Golden Formula—and establish self-knowledge on any subject we're interested in through contemplation. Then we won't have to worry about moving to safe areas. We will automatically find ourselves in the perfect location, in the perfect circumstances, and surrounded by the perfect group of people.

With the proper attitude and inner preparation, we can safely negotiate any changes that might occur. This is not a time of doom and gloom. Conversely, as the appearance of the Butterfly Children testifies, it is a time of great opportunity. 2012 looms large on the horizon. To the weary travelers that we are, it is a welcome beacon of hope!

*　　　　*　　　　*

Hope is a good thing,
maybe the best of things;
and no good thing ever dies.

– *"The Shawshank Redemption"*[37]

IN THE GARDEN OF THE GODS

Originally I intended to end this book after Chapter ten. It seemed like the proper place to leave off since I had covered 2012 and the Photon Belt as best I could. After several inner promptings, however, I decided to add this section on the Greater Reality. Since each person will approach the Absolute in a different way, I was reluctant to include any personal experiences; but once again I was overruled. If by doing so I am able to aid others in their quest for the 'ultimate secret,' then it has been worthwhile.

*   *   *

Although I haven't lived in southern Oregon for over a decade, I still return to Colliding Rivers a couple of times a year for answers and inspiration. It brings to mind a simpler, carefree time. But whenever I pass the site of the old cabin, a pain in my heart reminds me that the Chief is no longer there.

Our conversations at Colliding Rivers continued beyond the Christmas of 1987, well into the following summer. Our latter discussions ranged from living in this world to living in the moment. On several occasions we talked about meditation and the no-mind state. We also talked about the power of silence and, equally important, the power of words.

For example, the way we speak to ourselves and to the universe perpetuates the illusion that we are limited beings, separate from All That Is. We say to ourselves "I am a musician," when in reality we are the performer, the instrument, and the music itself. Better we should say "I AM a White Fire Being performing as a musician," or, "I AM the Divine experiencing how it feels to play music."

In September of 1988 my spiritual journey led me to Colorado, Idaho, and then to Canada before returning to college for a second time. My friendship with the Chief continued, but distance and my busy schedule proved to be substantial obstacles. After graduation my new career took me to Portland, Oregon, the *City of Roses*. One night I received a call around ten o'clock. It was the Chief.

He was moving to Arizona. The warmer climate would be better for Goldie's rheumatism, he told me. We talked for over an hour before saying goodbye. He said to be sure to look him up if I was ever in Arizona. I thanked him for the call... I also told him how much his friendship had meant to me over the years. It had truly been a priceless treasure. I'm glad I told him that.

Three years later I took a trip to the Southwest to see a childhood friend and his new wife; but mostly I drove down to see the Chief. I missed our conversations. A lot had happened in my life since I'd seen him last, and I was anxious to fill him in. To my disappointment, he was nowhere to be found. I checked first in Flagstaff, his original destination, and then in Sedona, but his name wasn't listed in either directory.

Knowing the Chief's dislike of cities, I wasn't surprised when I also came up empty in Phoenix and in Tucson.

Chief Dan George portrayed the wise, old, adopted grandfather of Dustin Hoffman in the movie, *Little Big Man*. While his appearance is different from the Chief's, his personality in the film is strikingly similar. Whenever Dustin Hoffman would reappear in his life, Chief Dan George's character would receive him with a broad smile and a cordial greeting: "My heart soars like a hawk to see you again, Little Big Man!" In like fashion, John Redstone's eyes always lit up each time we met for a discussion. It is no wonder I have rented *Little Big Man* countless times over the years.

Of all the fascinating things I learned from the Chief, it was not so much what he said that inspired me, it was what he was. He was a living example of the principles I had read about for many years. He radiated spirituality. He gave his full attention to the moment, no matter how insignificant that moment appeared to others. It was as if he was living that moment for God.

Aside from the instruction, can you imagine what it would be like to be around someone who never complained, who never found fault, someone who always accepted you unconditionally and treated you with great respect? Now I know firsthand why the students of Hazrat Khan, Yogananda, and Sawan Singh, the "Great Master," have expressed such honor and gratitude at the opportunity of spending time with such space-giving and enlightened beings.

In our many conversations, the Chief often stressed three things: 1) Whatever the mind of man can imagine must become reality, 2) There is always enough (because we create it), and 3) We are never alone. I am also grateful that he taught me about the Belief

System, and the significance of 2012. But even more importantly, the Chief awakened in me a higher aspiration.

As grand as it may seem, graduating from the third dimension is just another step on a very long path. To fulfill our destiny we must transcend duality; we must awaken from the dream worlds of Maya. Our ultimate goal is nothing less than the culmination of our spiritual journey as White Fire Beings. It is "The Mystery" revealed, the "Secret of the Ages" come to light, the final act in the play of Self-discovery—Self-actualization. It is nothing less than the ineffable, inexhaustible bliss of God-Realization. As stated in a little-known book called *The Shariyat-Ki-Sugmad*:

> The Sugmad [SOOG-mod] is what there is and all there is, so that no name can really be given IT except the poetic name of God. IT is neither old nor new, great nor small, shaped nor shapeless. Having no opposite, IT is what opposites have in common; It is the reason why there is no white without black and no form apart from emptiness. However, the Sugmad, as we know IT, has two parts—an inside and an outside. The inside is called Nirguna, which is to say that IT has no qualities and nothing can be said or thought about IT. The outside is called Saguna, which is to say that IT may be considered as eternal reality, consciousness and joy. This is the part that man knows and remembers after experiencing the God-Realization state.[1]

The *Shariyat-Ki-Sugmad* explains further:

> Because of Its joy in reaching this state, Soul is capable of enjoying Itself in play. This type of play is called Lila, and is like singing and dancing made up of sound,

silence, motion, and rest. In this kind of play Soul will lose Itself and find Itself in a game of hide and seek without beginning or end. This is the joy that orthodox religions speak about, but in the losing of Itself, It is obliterated; It forgets that It is forever the one and only reality and plays that It is the vast multitude of beings and things which make up this world. In finding Itself, It is remembered; It will discover again that It is forever the one behind the many, the trunk from which the branches of the tree grow— the tree itself. It knows again that Its seeming to be many is always maya, or illusion, art and magical powers.[2]

The Chief awakened in me the desire for God. Not an immature and angry God, but the God of Infinite Bliss, the One True Reality lost in a marvelous game of eternal hide and seek. Thinking about the Absolute, along with worship and devotion, only whets the appetite. We must transcend duality in order to discover the Nameless One.

Since meeting the Chief, I've caught fleeting glimpses of this Divine Being on rare occasions. Once in my mother's eyes as she departed from this world; another time peering out from behind a stranger's eyes in a marketplace in Puerto Vallarta, Mexico.

At other times I have experienced a sense of "connectedness" while strolling through old-growth forests, while skiing in virgin powder, while listening to classical music, and while watching the sun set over the Pacific from a sand dune with friends. More often, however, were the difficult times, when I felt isolated and alone, unworthy of God. But these dark nights generally led to a greater understanding of life. Humility was often an added bonus.

North Umpqua Highway, Oregon, 1988

One such turning point happened in the early fall of 1988, soon after my last visit with the Chief at his cabin. A decision to move to Denver initiated a strange cycle of events that tested my resolve and took me to the edge of my comfortable little universe.

Following an inner nudge and without much planning, I packed everything I owned in my aging sports car and left family and friends around ten o'clock on a rainy Saturday night. As I passed the city limits sign, I happened to glance at my odometer. It read 169,443. This was incredible. Only a week before, the Chief had mentioned that very number.

During a lengthy discussion of the Belief System he had interjected a seemingly unrelated statement about balance. At the time I had thought to myself how out of place the remark had seemed. The Chief mentioned in passing that everything in the physical universe balanced to a certain number. That number was 169,443! Without further explanation he returned to his topic. Now, as I drove east along the North Umpqua River toward the Cascade Range, I reflected on the curious statement. Why had this number now appeared in my life? My life was anything but balanced.

A thunderstorm pelted the North Umpqua basin, reducing the visibility of a moonless night. Prudence dictated pulling over. I had slept in my car before, but never with it fully loaded. Around midnight I remembered a rock ledge near a trailhead leading to a waterfall the Chief and I had visited twice before. On our last hike I had thought to myself how the ledge could provide protection in an emergency. Now, three months later, I found myself sloshing along the muddy trail toward the natural shelter.

My heart jumped as a deer bounded up the trail ahead of me, scattering loose rock with its hooves. How different the woods can be at night! I breathed a sigh of relief as the dark escarpment appeared in my flashlight beam twenty yards away. Susan Creek churned out a raucous welcome as I rolled out my sleeping bag, bumping my head on the four-foot ceiling. I thought of my friends sequestered in their safe and comfortable homes, their thermostats set at 70 degrees. What a different life I had chosen.

But even suffering with a mild case of the flu, the experience wasn't half-bad. As I lay awake marveling at the inauspicious beginning to my new life, a feeling of gratitude flooded through me. After all, I was dry... and a warm wave of love enveloped me like a soft cotton blanket. I remembered a passage from a book called *Stranger by the River,* an appropriate title for my present circumstance: "God loves and takes special care of those who love Him with all their heart and Soul."[3]

The next morning I was awakened by a single drop of rain splashing upon my forehead. This one drop had somehow penetrated my rock fortress. I awoke in a state of bliss. It was not just a raindrop intruding upon my dreams, it was a kiss from the Infinite gently awakening me to a new day.

What Colorado would have in store was still a mystery, but I hit the North Umpqua Highway that morning with renewed enthusiasm and a clearer sense of spiritual purpose. Without these two qualities it is difficult to reach the journey's end. Even more important is a strong desire for God. The spiritual path draws seekers from different backgrounds with varied motives. None are turned away. But many drop out along the way as Attar testifies in *The Conference of the Birds:*

In the end, only a small number of all this great company arrived at that sublime place to which the Hoopoe had led them. Of the thousands of birds, almost all had disappeared. Many had been lost in the ocean, others had perished on the summits of the high mountains, tortured by thirst; others had had their wings burnt and their hearts dried up by the fire of the sun; others were devoured by tigers and panthers; others died of fatigue in the deserts and in the wilderness, their lips parched and their bodies overcome by the heat; some went mad and killed each other for a grain of barley; others, enfeebled by suffering and weariness, dropped on the road unable to go further; others, bewildered by the things they saw, stopped where they were, stupefied; and many, who had started out from curiosity or pleasure, perished without an idea of what they had set out to find.[4]

Garden of the Gods, Fall of 1988

In Denver I took a job delivering packages with some old friends from high school who had moved to Colorado for the skiing. I was given a city map and two pieces of advice: "Park wherever you can, either legal or illegal," and, "yellow lights mean *go faster.*" After a couple of hectic months risking life and limb in the bustling streets, the driver for whom I was filling in returned. I was asked to stay, but my inner voice urged me to press on. This was not the reason for my Colorado excursion.

I had promised myself a leisurely day of sightseeing once my job had ended. When Saturday rolled around, I pointed my car south toward Colorado Springs and new vistas. At a gas station on the edge of that city, I reached for a cup of coffee. I'd had two cups already, my normal limit, but today I felt like living dangerously.

"No more coffee!" The startling impression caught me by surprise. How curious. I replaced the cup and paid for my gas.

"Where does this road go?" I asked. The cashier gave me an *everybody knows where this road goes* look, then pointed toward the huge road sign.

"Garden of the Gods," she replied indifferently.

"Of course, the Garden of the Gods," I mused. Perhaps a quiet stroll through a botanical garden was just what the doctor ordered after two stressful months of scanning maps, searching for street numbers, and running yellow lights. Why then, I asked myself, the growing sense of uneasiness?

A delivery from the preceding week came to mind as I sped toward the foothills. I'd been asked to pick up a package from a company called "Oracle," and then drop it off in "Golden," Colorado. On the way to the delivery point I had misread a street sign for Indiana Blvd. I had read it as "Indian" Blvd.

Instead of a serene garden of flowers, I found myself at the entrance to a lush green valley guarded by several towering rock formations. To my immediate right, one three hundred-fifty foot giant rose above the winding road leading to the park restaurant and observatory. The uneasy feeling continued as I climbed the wooden steps to the gift shop. I had purposely left my pen in my car, somehow hoping I'd have nothing to record. After purchasing a map describing the many formations, I embarked on a course down the middle path toward Cathedral Rock (not to be confused with the famous attraction by the same name in Sedona, Arizona).

"These Gateway Rocks," the brochure stated, "are composed of fine, beach-like sand." Since my vision of ancient Lemuria, I paid close attention whenever the word *beach* came up. For me, the word symbolized returning to my spiritual home. No wonder I was feeling uneasy. If I was correctly reading between the lines, my resolve was about to be tested. My eyes fell on a paragraph on the map marked 'Warning.'

"Every year some of the unwary must be rescued," it said. "Frequently others are hurt by falling, and occasionally one drops to his death. Such risky climbing should be undertaken only under expert guidance. Two or more climbers with proper equipment and previous registration at the GG Visitor Center is now a requirement for climbing." The advice made perfect sense to me.

The path veered abruptly to the right, depositing me at the base of a three hundred foot cliff. I tilted my head back and gazed straight up. As if on cue, words began to form in my mind from an unknown source: *"If these ancient rocks could speak, they would tell of the mysteries of God."*

Spellbound I waited, struggling to clear my mind of the confusion and fear generated by the initial shock. I realized that any interference could cloud my awareness should a lengthy discourse unfold. Only one more sentence followed, however. In the silence of the garden, the full impact of the statement hit me like a boulder: *"God-Realization awaits at the top of this rock!"*

Nervously I walked around the left side of the rock, searching for an accessible path. At a loss as to what to do, I studied the other tourists. Perhaps thirty people were wandering around the grounds, many with small children who played near the base of the rocks. Only two men, armed with the latest equipment, seemed interested in a serious climb.

A lady in her late fifties was standing about fifteen yards away, scanning the horizon. As the woman spoke to her husband, a message came through in the *Golden-tongued Wisdom*.[5] "The path is any way you'd like to go!"

I noticed that the rock behind me was even taller than Cathedral Rock... and a nice safe trail offered an easy ascent. Perhaps God-Realization was at the top of this rock, too! I switched my sights to this modest challenge.

It proved to be a simple climb. I wasn't quite to the top, but probably close enough, I speculated. According to the brochure, this rock was called "The South Gateway with the Indian Head." I closed my eyes and tried to focus on the task at hand—stilling the mind. But my thoughts kept drifting over to the rock cliff directly across from me.

An hour passed as I sang the word HU, the secret name of God. I was accompanied by a howling wind that sprang up from nowhere. A strange loneliness seeped into my consciousness like an ancient underground spring, silently undermining the sandstone beneath me.

Suddenly the wind died down. Peace should now regain its claim on the Garden of the Gods, I thought. Instead, an unnerving sound rippled through the silence, causing me to shudder involuntarily. It was the cry of a crow, my totem. It had come from the top of Cathedral Rock.

Reluctantly, I descended the South Gateway and studied the map, hoping to discover a tip as to how I might scale the cliff before me. In the background, the rock known as "The Sleeping Indian" offered no advice. A single dark cloud hovered in the aquamarine sky; coincidentally, it was directly above Cathedral Rock. I remembered that every silver lining has a dark cloud attached to it, as I reached for a handhold. The warning on the map came back to me: "Such risky climbing should be undertaken only under expert guidance." It seemed like a good time to call upon my Higher Self, the Chief, and any other "experts" who might be listening.

Not until I was well into the steep climb did I realize that I was on my own. I'd been given a choice. "The path is any way you'd like to go," I'd been told. I'd also been shown in black and white that risk would be involved. Now I only prayed that I wouldn't be the "one" who dropped to his death.

Carefully, and ever so slowly, I clawed my way from handhold to handhold. To an experienced climber the ascent would have been a great adventure. For me, however, every inch was sheer agony. To make matters worse, my great fear of heights surfaced and was my constant companion every inch of the way.

At last I spotted a narrow ledge about ten feet above me. Only another inaccessible fifteen feet lay beyond. On the way up I'd spotted several places where the sandstone had given way and had tumbled to the valley floor. Despite this, I forced myself to climb out on the ledge. My mind protested, but I pushed beyond it. Blood oozed from a cut on the back of my right hand, as the weakness in my knees increased. I cast an anxious glance to the ground, nearly three hundred feet below. One wrong move could prove fatal. Paradoxically, I had never felt so alive. I was totally living in the moment.

Karl Wallenda, the patriarch of "The Flying Wallendas," once made a similar observation. When asked about his choice of careers he replied, "On the wire I'm alive. All the rest is 'just waiting.'"[6]

Very carefully I retraced my steps. The descent was every bit as hazardous as the trip up, yet the fact that I was moving toward safety made it many times easier. Had there been no tourists I might have kissed the ground, so great was my joy upon reaching the bottom. But I'd just done a brave thing. Why tarnish it with undue sentiment? I felt like someone who had just battled a serious illness and had won good health again. My knees were still weak, and a touch of nausea had followed me down, but aside from that I was in fine shape.

After buying half a dozen postcards to commemorate my triumph over death, I adjourned to the restaurant to enjoy a victory meal. The room was crowded and brimming with life. From a large picture window I glanced out across the quiet meadow as I unwrapped a sandwich. What I saw made my mouth drop open in disbelief. Someone was standing on the very pinnacle of Cathedral Rock and was waving in my direction! The man wore no traditional climbing gear. I didn't know who he was or why he was waving, but I knew I had to go back up.

Such was the path I'd chosen. There are few words to describe the second ascent. Perhaps that's the way it should be, since the next person's journey will no doubt be different. I never did find out who'd been waving from the top.

The following Monday I left Colorado. I'd met several new friends in Denver and I'd seen some new country...and I was alive. I left town with a keen sense of gratitude; yet it was tempered by an indescribable feeling of emptiness. My second trip to the summit had brought no flashes of Cosmic Consciousness, no sense of Oneness, no bliss, only vague premonitions of things to come. Moreover, it had left me with an indiscernible longing for someone or something; maybe even somewhere. This yearning had been buried deep in my Soul prior to my experience in the Garden of the Gods. Now it was only a hairbreadth away, just below the threshold of consciousness. I could almost touch it.

It excited me. It confounded me. It haunted me. It made me feel like a man living in the wrong time... or the wrong place, a stranger in a strange land. Perhaps that was it: I was longing for home.

*   *   *

Deep inside there's a memory
I can't quite embrace,
a yearning for somewhere
I almost can place,

when we traveled as One
at the start of the play;
you dressed as the moon,
and I dressed the same.

    – the author

SOMEWHERE ALONG THE WAY

<u>Sun Valley, Idaho, Fall of 1988</u>

My return trip to Oregon was delayed by yet another unusual happenstance. It led to a reunion of sorts, a meeting with someone from my distant past. I was anxious to see the Chief, but other than that, I saw no reason to hurry home. Wyoming held no special interest for me, but when I crossed the Idaho border I slowed down a bit.

Since I'd been interested in skiing for a number of years, I'd done considerable reading about the mountains of Idaho. When the Sun Valley exit came into view, I decided that a detour was in order. The first snowfall was still a month or so away and the roads were clear. In the back of my mind I was looking for a home. Why not a ski town? This was "Hemingway country," a rugged wilderness nourished by the Salmon River. The famous author had found ample inspiration in this part of Idaho. What better place for an aspiring writer?

After spending several hours browsing through the quaint shops that lined the main street in Sun Valley, however, I realized that my home lay elsewhere. I grabbed a sandwich on the way up to the mountain, where barren ski runs cut narrow paths through islands of green. I roamed around awhile, planning out the remainder of my day. If I left immediately, I could reach Boise by suppertime. I could spend a leisurely evening with friends who had recently relocated there.

That was my plan. But when I came to the stop sign at the Boise turnoff, something made me hesitate. For a good half-minute I sat poised at the crossroads, gazing blankly toward the mountains north of Sun Valley. Not a thought crossed my mind the entire thirty seconds. Then, without a clue as to why I would set off for the wilderness this late in the afternoon, I abruptly turned left. Boise would have to wait.

The view from the winding road flanking the Salmon River was truly breathtaking in places, yet I kept wondering "why?" Why was my inner guidance leading me further and further from civilization? What was the point? I could still make Boise by ten, my mind protested. Why not turn around? The answer to that question came through loud and clear: "Keep going!"

Finally I relaxed and put the mystery on hold. I sat back in my seat and enjoyed the adventure. As mile after mile passed beneath my wheels, the mighty Salmon River grew smaller and smaller. Finally it transformed from a treacherous, raging river into a tiny, playful stream, shallow enough to wade across in places. My attention was drawn to a roadside marker. "Point of Interest Ahead," it announced.

As I approached the vehicle turnout, a small sign came into view. It elicited the strangest sensation. It was at once a feeling of great anticipation coupled with great trepidation. In every fiber of my being I knew that whatever was printed on that sign was the reason I had driven several hours out of my way.

Timidly, I rolled down the window and slowly read the words aloud: *HEADWATERS OF THE RIVER OF NO RETURN.* This was the name Ernest Hemingway had given the Salmon River. I didn't know why he'd called it that, but I did know that I'd just been given a great opportunity. In the symbolic language, I was being asked to return to the Source, to the Unchanging Ocean of Ecstasy, my home.

As I drove along a cliff overlooking the beautiful blue river, my inner senses suddenly opened. Without warning, I found myself gazing out upon a shimmering River of Golden Light. It flowed out at a forty-five degree angle into the heavens. The river started as a trickle, flowing from my own heart in a wave of joy. It spread out in an ever-expanding current of love, stretching beyond eyesight, beyond time and space, and into infinity. I remembered my vision of ancient Lemuria, as those oft-recalled words rang in my ears: *"The River of God flows from the heart of every creature."*

The vision lasted several moments, and in those golden moments I realized that all the great experiences I'd sought meant nothing when compared to a single moment in this stream of love. As it began to fade, a message flowed into my consciousness on a wave of bliss: "The more you are aware that the light of God centers within you, the more you will become aware that the light is thy very self."

That night around ten I rented a small cabin just south of Sun Valley. Still stunned by the day's events, I tossed and turned on the hard, uneven mattress.

What a strange and wonderful cycle had begun when my car odometer had clicked over to 169,443.

My thoughts drifted back to my mother. I remembered a collection of verses called *Golden Moments* I'd given her when she'd become ill. The verses weren't all that great. I'd been attracted to it because of the cover. It featured a photograph of a Hawaiian sunset with a river of gold shimmering upon the sea.

As I drifted into the twilight area between waking consciousness and sleep, the silhouette of a man suddenly appeared in the distance. There was no setting whatsoever, only a formless grey void... and the ghost-like being now approaching at a brisk walk. Stopping a few feet away, he smiled warmly. Although he was wearing a maroon robe instead of the toga I had first seen him in, I recognized his features immediately. Again I tingled with anticipation. Somewhere deep inside, the question I knew he was about to ask echoed through distant and forgotten corridors of my mind.

"Would you like to know where the Golden River ends?" he finally asked. It was the same question I'd been asked on the beach in Lemuria seventy thousand years before... only now I knew how to answer. For whatever reason, I had missed the opportunity to return home in that bygone day. But now I was ready.

Butchart Gardens, Victoria B.C., Canada,
Spring of 1989

Once back in Oregon I picked up old threads of existence. But now nothing seemed right. The things I used to enjoy—skiing, hiking, softball, movies, socializing—had all lost their allure. Even old friends acted differently around me. I didn't fit in. I had no direction in life, nor was I especially happy. A return to college wasn't the answer, but at least it was a change. Before settling in for another two years of technical school in the fall of 1989, however, I went on a vacation to Victoria, British Columbia. It was really a vision quest.

My image of the Butchart Gardens had always been one of rainbow-colored flowers arranged in artistic designs, but even clothed in the basic green of early spring, the sanctuary exuded an air of dignity. It was a tranquil place, worthy of its acclaim.

As I sat alone on a park bench overlooking a section known as the *Sunken Garden,* my eyes fell on a passage in the program describing the various areas and pathways in the renowned attraction. "You now have two choices," I read. One path meandered through exotic flora representing many countries. The other path offered a more direct route, but with few attractions. I chose the former. Both led to the same place, the Rose Garden.

A stray image breezed through my consciousness like a wayward kite, and for the briefest moment I was carried to a place far away. In this dreamlike setting I heard someone ask, "What path have you chosen?"

"The path of the heart," was the reply. A haunting feeling of deja vu followed me down the trail as I recalled a familiar verse from a Robert Frost poem:

> I shall be telling this with a sigh
> Somewhere ages and ages hence;
> Two roads diverged in a wood, and I—
> I took the one less traveled by,
> And that has made all the difference.[1]

Some interesting things happened at the Rose Garden, where roses would bloom later in the spring. I noticed a multitude of thorns awaiting their arrival. My attention was drawn to a small sign near an irrigation faucet, to my right: "This water is impure."

Recently I'd read that nothing impure could stand before the sight of God.

I passed beneath the archway of thorns and stood before the entrance to the perfect circle of green grass at the pathway's end. It symbolized the culmination of my long spiritual journey. When this auspicious event would actually take place was anybody's guess. Unfortunately, I knew what the thorns symbolized: pain and sacrifice.

As I awoke in a hotel room in Victoria the next morning, I found the fragment of a poem on my lips. The verse, called "Rain on the Roses," was of unknown origin. It had an appropriate ending for someone struggling to find his place in the cosmos:

A kiss hello, then a kiss goodbye;
from the rose and the thorn flow a sad, sweet life.

Horseheaven Creek, Umpqua National Forest, 1996

In every moment of creation love finds expression through the principle of Rhythmic Balanced Interchange. One polarity gives its energy to its opposite, which in turn, re-gives itself to the other; therefore, creation is first and foremost an act of love. The Chief often advised, "If you want to know love, immerse yourself in giving." But success also necessitates learning to receive. These two are forever intertwined.

One weekend, while driving up the North Umpqua Highway, I remembered an abandoned cabin located near the headwaters of Horseheaven Creek, about ten miles northwest of Steamboat Falls. Several years before first meeting the Chief, I had explored the region with an old friend who had introduced me to gold panning. I'd planned to spend the night at a campground further upriver, but an inner nudge prompted me to seek out the cabin instead.

Now, as I hiked along the ravaged banks of the stream, I found that little had changed since my initial visit. Only a new beaver dam now backed up the tiny stream in one section, forming a glistening, emerald pool. The waterway had once been the jewel of the Bohemia Basin, famous for its gold rush in the early 1900's. When the gold had run out, however, title to Horseheaven Creek had reverted back to Mother Nature through "quitclaim."

The first sight of the cabin brought a rush of nostalgia, although the dwelling appeared to be in the same state of disrepair. I found a large section of the roof missing now, and the cast iron stove had slipped one leg toward freedom through the rotting floor. The old mattress was still spread out in the darkest corner, but mildew had set in from years of dampness. Broken bottles lay outside the opening in the wall where the window had been. Even in its present state, I decided to call the shelter "home" for an evening.

At one time I had asked God to bring people into my life to teach me about love. These were the kind and simple people, scattered like wildflowers throughout the unknown meadows of the world. I remembered them now as I sat amid the simple daisies and cheerful bluebonnets overlooking Horseheaven Creek. Buttercups grew among them in random patterns. It looked as though some traveler had paused here, only long enough to scatter a few handfuls of seeds to the wind before moving on.

A tiny blue flower radiated life at my feet. Its most noticeable quality was its insignificance when compared to the buttercups surrounding it. I was probably the first person who had even taken the time to cast an appreciative glance in its direction. Who would love this abandoned flower of God?

I had closed my eyes for but a moment, when into my inner vision stepped the teacher I had met so long ago, the adept I simply called "the Lemurian." He was clad in white, in a robe perhaps woven from daydream images, but I could see that he was carrying a copper watering can and a silver gardening tool. With infinite tenderness he sprinkled a few drops of water on the tiny blue flower at his feet.

"Who would love this special flower of God?" he asked, looking up. "Why, I would!"

After a light dinner of dried fruit and nuts, I cleared a space on the dusty cabin floor, thankful at least for an unobstructed view of the sky. Our surroundings often reflect our innermost states of consciousness. As I was falling asleep, I wondered why fate had drawn me back to Horseheaven Creek and the neglected cabin with all its problems. By morning I would have my answer.

That night in the dream state I found myself back in the gold rush days with the Chief. He was holding a miner's pick and a large bag of gold dust. We were inspecting the cabin, discussing the possibility of making it livable again. All in all, I thought to myself, the cabin had seen its share of problems.

"This cabin has only one problem," mused the Chief, as if thinking out loud. "Worthiness! Yes, that's it," he said, as if he'd just made a great discovery. "The problem is *worthiness*.

"It's like us," he marveled, in the same self-directed tone. "We spend hours concentrating on opening our heart and giving, but it's all for naught. We've lost the ability to receive.

"This old, abandoned cabin is a reflection of our issues of abandonment. It follows that the state of disrepair is symbolic of judgments we've formed from being abandoned.

"See how this feels," he replied, turning to acknowledge my presence for the first time: 'I've been abandoned, therefore I must be unworthy—unworthy of prosperity, unworthy of happiness, unworthy of love.' How can we hope to receive the greatest treasure of all," he asked shaking his head, "if we feel unworthy to receive it? How can we receive 'the Golden Heart?'"

As I pondered the Chief's question I noticed that my surroundings had changed. I saw a pair of large, illuminated hands suspended in a dark void. I knew they were *my* hands. A stream of gold dust was pouring down from the heavens, most of it falling through my open fingers. "If I have *my* needs met," I heard myself thinking, "others must go without."

"Notice the size of the stream of gold dust flowing beneath your palms," urged a soft voice coming from the ethers. I recognized the voice as belonging to the Lemurian sage. After I had done so, he continued.

"Now, close your fingers." As I closed my fingers, the stream beneath my cupped hands stopped flowing, while the gold filled my palms. Once full, however, the gold overflowed and the stream beneath resumed.

"Again." my teacher directed. "Notice the size of the stream of gold dust flowing beneath your hands."

I got the point. The two streams were exactly the same! By receiving from life I was in no way diminishing the supply below. All that was needed was to feel worthy enough to close my fingers. As the dream ended, I heard the now familiar voice of the Lemurian. "The beaver is content," he stated, "because he has learned to receive. He takes what he needs without reducing the flow of abundance to others downstream. For this reason he is called 'the Worthy One.'"

I awoke the next morning to the intoxicating fragrance of lilac and honeysuckle. Retracing my steps, I stopped beside the emerald pool to eat some granola before hitting the main road. I took with me a new appreciation for the beaver.

*   *   *

Later that summer, while hiking along a placid section of the North Umpqua not far from Steamboat Creek, I sat down on a beached log near the water's edge. I happened to notice a small shell nestled among the dull, grey rocks. As I picked up the gold, heart-shaped shell I felt a sudden thrill of excitement. Resting in my hand was an elusive treasure, one the hordes of fortune hunters had somehow overlooked. It was a *Golden Heart*. Of what use a fragile, gold-colored shell would be to anyone, I couldn't begin to guess... but I didn't have to guess, for a short verse formed in my mind. It was clear that the Golden Heart was a blessing from God:

THE GOLDEN HEART

To possess this heart is not to possess it,
for the Golden Heart is the giver of life.
One may only possess it who gives it away.

From hand to hand,
from heart to heart,
throughout eternity it must freely pass.
Only God decides who is worthy of this treasure.
Only God knows the holder
of the Golden Heart!

Butchart Gardens, Victoria B.C., 1998

We live our lives in circles within circles, in cycles within cycles. Thus it was inevitable that, nine years after my first visit, I would return to my spiritual home here on Earth.

*   *   *

A light mist was falling on the daffodils the day I returned to Victoria. Late springtime in the Butchart Gardens was as beautiful as I'd imagined it would be. The air was sweet with the fragrance of rainbow-colored flowers. It was a literal paradise, yet I found myself slipping into a melancholy mood as I climbed the tulip-lined path to the Rose Garden.

I remembered other springs, the bouquets of wildflowers I'd picked for my mom, and the baseball practices with my dad and brother. I remembered teenage romances and childhood playmates... and the Chief. They were gone now, even the rustic cabin at Colliding Rivers. Perhaps Thomas Wolfe was right, maybe you can't go home.[2]

I paused beneath the latticework archway where roses were blooming in great profusion. Following an inner nudge, I picked a single, yellow rose, growing apart from the rest. Before me lay the perfect circle of green grass at the pathway's end. I glanced back one last time at the long road over which I'd come. Funny, I couldn't tell if years had passed, or centuries... or was it but a single moment?

With my inner vision I detected a radiant being approaching from the opposite side of the circle. As he crossed the neatly trimmed grass in graceful strides, I could see that it was my teacher, the Lemurian, the one being who had never abandoned me. He wore a navy blue Hawaiian shirt, tan slacks, and matching leather sandals. A yellow garland of plumeria adorned his neck. Flashing a compassionate smile, he stopped a few feet away.

My heart raced. There were so many things I wanted to say. I owed him so much, yet for all the world, the only gift I could think of to express my love and gratitude was a single, yellow rose. As I stood before him holding the flower, I could see the great Ocean of Love shining through his eyes from the depths of his Soul, that great Ocean of Light that was my home!

Waves of bliss swelled in my heart, then overflowed in a great, Golden River of Light and Sound that echoed to the furthest shores of my being. Upon the crests of this river my imaginings took shape as an indivisible whole reflected Itself into seeming multiplicity. Individual spirals of two-way electric light played upon the backdrop of time and space, only to surrender their individuality to an Ocean of Stillness once their purpose was fulfilled. I saw all of creation as an expression of love, a vehicle for giving through Rhythmic Balanced Interchange between unbalanced pairs of opposites.

This glimpse into the Absolute revealed the truth about my life as a human being. It was only an illusion—the play of Maya. My life on Earth was nothing more than a dream. And it wasn't even my dream; it was God's dream! All the other dreams I'd called "my past" existed in the stillness of this Golden Moment, as well. Past and future had no meaning here.

In this heightened state of awareness it was all so clear. My consciousness was everywhere; yet it was also rooted in the physical world. I was timeless; yet I was experiencing time. I was awake; yet I was also standing in the Rose Garden, dreaming I was awake. I heard someone ask a question.

"Don't you recognize me?" the Lemurian asked. His voice sounded distant and dreamlike. My senses told me that I was standing before my teacher in the garden, but my consciousness was also somewhere else.

This dual consciousness was very confusing to my space/time-conditioned mind. It lashed out in desperation for a familiar anchor-point. But all it could grasp was the Lemurian's features, now swimming before my inner vision.

I must have looked funny standing there beneath the roses with a blank expression on my face, for the adept laughed softly. I struggled to hold on to the scene before me, but it was no use. From somewhere very far away came the faint sound of waves breaking upon a shore...

*   *   *

"Don't you recognize me?" my teacher repeated, rising from the foot of the palm. With a fluid motion, he brushed the sand from his light blue toga. The Lemurian sun was now only a half-disc shimmering above the horizon.

"Of course I do, Master," I answered with a sleepy smile. "I'm sorry. I must have been daydreaming. I picked this for you." I held out the gift I'd brought him, trying to remember where I'd found the yellow rose.

"I picked this for you," I said, "somewhere along the way." My master's eyes beamed with joy.

"Have you been waiting long?" I asked, fearing that I was late for our appointment.

"Not long," he answered reassuringly. "You're right on time. Shall we go?"

I studied the small sailboat as we walked to the water's edge, wondering if it would be sturdy enough for such an adventuresome voyage.

"Home," I said quietly, feeling the word vibrate to the depths of my being. "Home is where the heart is."

"What a beautiful thought!" exclaimed the great being at my side, turning to face me.

I smiled. "It just came to me. Is it far?" I asked. "Is home far away?"

The Lemurian gazed out upon the shimmering River of Golden Light dancing upon the ocean. "Not far," he answered softly. "I know a short-cut."

EPILOGUE

I placed the finished manuscript on the table and went for a walk along the wind-blown beach. It was five-thirty in the morning, and the first rays of the sun were just beginning to light up the Pacific. A single set of footprints led down the shoreline ahead of me.

The eternal rhythm of the waves had a hypnotic effect, and for the briefest moment my mind experienced a sense of confusion. For the briefest moment I was floating free, drifting forward in my imagination. The footprints stretched out ahead of me as before, but the water had changed ever so slightly. Now, the warm Golden Light appeared to be coming from the Ocean, Itself.

The footprints suddenly stopped at the edge of the Golden Sea of liquid Light. I looked up to find the Lemurian's all-knowing gaze studying me. He smiled as I approached, and again I felt the familiar wave of love enfold me. "You know where you are, don't you?" he asked.

"Yes, Dear Heart," I answered happily. "I'm home!"

FORTUNE UNDEFINED

If I was the Master of Illusion,
   and you had a fortune undefined,
I'd scatter your thoughts
   into yesterday and tomorrow,
then I'd hide your fortune in this moment of time.

For who'd ever know of this moment,
   who'd ever know of this rhyme,
who'd ever know save the children
   who are living and breathing at this moment
from the fortune undefined.

           – Jack McCoy[1]

ACKNOWLEDGMENTS

My special thanks go out to Judith Irwin for her insightful initial edit. This was done at considerable sacrifice, as her own plate was brimming at the time. Barbara Hand Clow also took time out of her busy schedule to review the manuscript. She suggested a content change that greatly improved the work.

I extend my gratitude to Brenda Evans for her creative graphics and for typesetting the book; to Cheryl Fontaine for additional graphics and support; to Leslie Dyer for her comprehensive final edit; and to Karla Joy McMechan for the many hours she spent helping me refine the second printing.

I would also like to thank my proofreaders, Anita Krotz and Sally Thomas, and the following people for their material contributions: Gene & Wanda Davis, Jamie Davis, Sheree Gamelin, Vicki Gooch, James Hall, Daniel Lang, David Loitz, Jack McCoy, and Linda McCoy Summer.

NOTES

<u>Front cover (Earth quote)</u>: Robert Ghost Wolf, *Winds of Change* (Mistyc House, 1997) p. 6.

<u>Introduction:</u>
1. Term "Photon Belt" was coined by the astronomer, Paul Otto Hesse, as noted by David Icke in *The Biggest Secret* (Bridge of Love Publications, 1999) pp. 476-477.
2. There are 2,160 of these 104,000-year cycles in one 225-million-year Galactic Orbit. (Ref: Barbara Hand Clow, *The Pleiadian Agenda: A New Cosmology for the Age of Light,* Bear & Co., 1995, pp. 49, 105.)
3. Jay Weidner and Vincent Bridges, *A Monument to the End of Time: Alchemy, Fulcanelli, and the Great Cross* (Aethyrea Books, 1999) p. 173.
4. From a discourse by the Chief.

<u>Chapter 1: The Dragon's Breath and the Valley of Man</u>
1. Ken Adachi, "The New World Order: An Overview," at www.educate-yourself.org/nwo.
2. Dr. John Coleman is the author of *The Committee of 300* (WIR Publishing, 1997). Quote is from David Icke, *Biggest Secret,* back cover.
3. Three techniques for Soul Travel are given by Paul Twitchell in *The Spiritual Notebook* (Illuminated Way Press, 1971) pp. 72-77.
4. Twitchell, *Spiritual Notebook,* p. 75.
5. James Churchward, *The Lost Continent of MU* (Brotherhood of Life/BE Books, 1926) pp. 1, 6, 51.
6. David Childress, *Lost Cities of Ancient Lemuria and the Pacific,* quoted in "Lemuria," *Crystalinks,* www.crystalinks.com.
7. Brother Philip, *Secret of the Andes* (Leaves of Grass Press, 1976) p. 8.
8. Churchward, *Lost Continent of MU,* pp. 52, 92-94.
9. Churchward, *Lost Continent of MU,* p. 59.
10. Adapted from a verse at http://watercolor.net.

Chapter 2: Behold: The Golden Age

1. Parables, stories, and conversations from this weeklong hike with John Redstone are detailed in *Porcupines at the Dance: Parables and Stories from Colliding Rivers.* (See www.SusanCreek.com.)

2. Some ancient calendars claim that our journey around the Central Sun takes 24,000 years rather than 26,000 years. Source: www.sanskritmantra.com/brahma.

3. David Icke, *...and the truth shall set you free* (Bridge of Love Publications, 1999) p. 483.

4. Mary Carroll Nelson, *Beyond Fear: A Toltec Guide to Freedom and Joy; The Teachings of Don Miguel Ruiz* (Council Oak Books, Tulsa & San Francisco, 1997) p. 31.

5. Adrian Gilbert and Maurice Cotterell, *The Mayan Prophecies* (Element Books Limited, Great Britain, 1995) inside cover.

6. Icke, *Biggest Secret,* p. 471.

7. Robert Ghost Wolf makes a case that our calendars are really five years behind in *Winds of Change,* p. 159. Glenn Kimball claims that our modern calendars are seven years off in *Hidden Politics of the Crucifixion* (Ancient Manuscripts Publishing, 1998) p. 35.

8. In 63 B.C., 700,000 ancient scrolls were lost at Alexandria, Egypt. (Ref: Kimball, *Hidden Politics of the Crucifixion.*) It is claimed that the controlling elite, prior to the fire, stole most of the valuable manuscripts. Many lie hidden beneath the Vatican to this day.

9. According to Carlos Barrios, the Mayans speak of a 52-year cycle of transition beyond 2012. John Redstone also believed that a 50-year Overlap Zone existed on the far side of 2012.

10. Gregg Braden, *Awakening to Zero Point* (Radio Bookstore Press, 1993) p. 98. Adaptation from *The Emerald Tablets of Thoth.*

Chapter 3: Journey of the White Fire Beings

1. Many believe these beings are the Anunnaki, a race originally from Orion. Reportedly they came here from Nibiru about 450,000 years ago. Nibiru is thought to be a planet located between Mars and Jupiter that enters our solar system every 3600 years. (Ref: Clow, *Pleiadian Agenda,* p. 274.) Zecharia Sitchin, translator of the Sumerian Tablets, also believes that the Anunnaki came from Nibiru as noted in *The Biggest Secret* by David Icke, p. 5.

2. Paul Twitchell, *Dialogues with the Master* (Illuminated Way Press, 1970) p. 40. "Prit" (pronounced and often spelled "PREET" in English) is from Sanskrit *priti,* meaning "love, affection, joy." (Sir Monier Monier-Williams, *Sanskrit-English Dictionary,* Oxford, England, Clarendon Press, 1960, p. 711.)

   Kal comes from the Sanskrit for the color "black" and is used to refer to dark clouds, night, snakes, various evil spirits, as well as the kali-yuga, or "dark ages" we are currently in (Monier-Williams, p. 277). The personification of the Kal power has been known by many names throughout history: Satan, the Devil, Beelzebub, Moloch, etc. Here it is referred to as the "Kal Power."

3. Twitchell, *Dialogues,* p. 40.

4. Paul Twitchell wrote about these archetypal experiences, calling them "nidanas" in *The ECK-Vidya: Ancient Science of Prophecy* (Illuminated Way Press, 1972) pp. 79-81.

5. T. S. Elliot, "Little Gidding," No. 4 of *Four Quartets.*

Chapter 4: Secrets of Creation

1. T. Lobsang Rampa, *The Cave of the Ancients* (Ballantine Books, 1963) p. 27. *The Third Eye,* published by Doubleday in 1956, was Rampa's biggest seller.

2. Hazrat Khan, *The Sufi Message of Hazrat Inayat Khan, Vol. II.: The Mysticism of Sound* (Barrie and Jenkins, London, 1962, 1973) p. 164.
3. Paramahansa Yogananda, *Autobiography of a Yogi* (Self-Realization Fellowship, Twelfth Edition, 1993) p. 320.
4. Yogananda, *Autobiography,* p. 318.
5. Yogananda, *Autobiography,* p. 320.
6. Walter Russell, *The Secret of Light* (University of Science and Philosophy, Third edition, 1947) p. 241. www.philosophy.com; 800-882-5683.
7. Russell, *Secret of Light,* p. 241.
8. Russell, *Secret of Light,* p. 224.
9. The Chief estimated that thought travels at approximately 10 billion miles/second on the Golden Thread.
10. Twitchell, *Spiritual Notebook,* p. 106. According to Twitchell, Soul is able to hear these Inner Sounds when linked to the Audible Lifestream through initiation. (Ref: *Spiritual Notebook,* pp. 42, 72-77, 153.)
11. The old English word "God," meaning "Supreme Being," dates from the old German word *Got,* and from Old Icelandic *Godh,* or *Gudh.* The Indo-Germanic base *gheu / ghu* means "to invoke," and "to pour" *(Barnhart Dictionary of Etymology).* The "h" in ancient Sanskrit becomes "gh" in the Indo-Germanic language. The idea of worship is reflected in the Germanic word *ghu,* as in the Sanskrit *hu (An Etymological Dictionary of the English Language).*

   Hoo, in the ancient Hawaiian language, is often attached as a prefix meaning "causation," or "to make." (Max Free Long, *The Secret Science Behind Miracles,* DeVORSS & CO., 1979, p. 396.) In the Naacal Writings, which contain fragments of the Sacred Inspired Writings of Lemuria, there is a simple circular glyph (Hun) that reads, "The Creator is One" *(The Children of MU,* by James Churchward).

The word *HU* has been poetically called "the breath of God." The concept of "pouring forth" and "returning to" perhaps most accurately reflects the true nature of the sacred and powerful word HU, the secret name of God.

12. Khan, *Sufi Message, Vol. II.,* p. 64.

13. Khan, *Sufi Message, Vol. II.,* p. 64. References to HU and the Vairagi (pronounced Vie-RAH-gee) are also found in Twitchell's writings. He states that HU is the ancient, secret name of God, which has been handed down through the ages by the ECK Masters, who are members of the secret brotherhood, the Ancient Order of the Vairagi (*ECK-Vidya,* p. 38).

   Harold Klemp, a modern-day Vairagi Master and successor to Paul Twitchell, lives in the Midwestern United States: www.eckankar.org/Harold, 1-800-LoveGod. NOTE: Two versions of the "HU Song" CD are available through the ECKANKAR website and phone number listed above.

   According to Khan, *"Aluk"* (pronounced *ah-LOOK*) is one of the sacred words that the Vairagi adepts use in their chants. He says it derives from *"al"* meaning "the," and *"Haq"* meaning "truth," or "The Truth." Therefore, Aluk refers to "God, the source from which all comes." If we divide *Haq* into two parts, its assonant sounds become *hu* and *ek; hu* signifying God, or truth, and *ek* in Hindustani meaning one.

14. Twitchell, *Spiritual Notebook,* p. 106.

15. Khan, *Sufi Message, Vol. II.,* p. 63.

16. The electronic keynote is sometimes called our "cosmic signature," or "resonance signature" by the Chief and by Walter Russell *(Secret of Light).*

17. Ruth Montgomery, *A World Beyond* (Fawcett Crest Books, 1972).

18. Edgar Cayce prediction, listed in "Prophesies About the New Millenium," 11/30/98: www.greatdreams.com/proph.htm.

19. Some believe that 2012 is also the end-point of the Universal Outbreath. (Ref: Ken Carey, *The*

Starseed Transmissions, Uni-Sun Books, 1982, p. 17.)

20. Ghost Wolf, *Winds of Change,* p. 180.
21. Post-cataclysm maps are available from a great many people including futurist, Gordon-Michael Scallion, and from Lori Toye, who claims to have worked with ascended masters on her *I AM America* map. Their respective websites are: www.matrixinstitute.com and www.iamamerica.com.
22. Gregg Braden, *The Isaiah Effect* (Harmony Books, New York, 2000) p. 84.

Chapter 5: Understanding the Seedbed

1. Robert Allen, *Creating Wealth* (Simon and Schuster, New York, 1983) p. 294. Quoted by Karl Marx in *Das Kapital;* originally an old proverb.
2. Ki energy is also known as life-force energy when it flows through the body.
3. Bruce Lee, *Tao of Jeet Kune Do* (Ohara Publications, 1975) p. 200.

Chapter 6: The Mirror of Life and the Golden Formula

1. According to the Chief, our sphere of influence was once 100 feet.
2. Braden, *Isaiah Effect,* pp. 21-22.
3. A number of methodologies specialize in the release of trapped emotions such as fear, anger, guilt, etc. When researching for these practitioners, look for key words such as "emotional release," "Release Work," "trapped feelings," and "Emotional Freedom Technique" (EFT).

Chapter 7: The Mechanics of Non-Resistance

1. Dennis Cuddy, Ph.D., *Secret Records Revealed* (Hearthstone Publications, 1994) p. 24.
2. Coleman, *Committee of 300,* pp. 159, 161.
3. Cuddy, *Secret Records Revealed,* pp. 27-28.

4. The Jeff Rense Radio Program is a good place to start: www.rense.com.
5. Al Bielek, lecture/videotape; Yelm, Washington, circa 1996. Also see: Al Bielek, "The Interviews," *Orion Technology and Other Secret Projects;* www.freezone.org/mc/e_conv04.
6. Jeff Rense, *Sightings Radio Show,* KOTK, Portland, Oregon, 3/16/01.
7. Barry Lynes, *The Cancer Cure That Worked,* (Marcus Books, Canada, 1987). Available only in Canada. The information presented in this book was taken from a photocopy.
8. Adelle Davis states that blood cholesterol levels are not raised by the consumption of eggs. (Ref: *Let's Get Well,* The New American Library, 1972, pp. 57, 58.) See also, "Cholesterol, Lipitor, and Big Government: The Terror Campaign Against Us All," Karen DeCoster; www.karendecoster.com.
9. Gene Davis, *Where We Are on the Cosmic Clock* (Life Research Foundation, 1987) p. 121.
10. Carl Bode, *The Portable Thoreau* (Penguin Books, 1947) p. 109.
11. Davis, *Cosmic Clock,* p. 108.
12. The high feeling derived from the consumption of alcohol is from oxygen being burned in the brain. (Ref: Ed McCabe, *Oxygen Therapies,* Energy Publications, 1988, p. 86.)

Chapter 8: Aquarius, The "Water-Bearer"
1. Bode, *Portable Thoreau,* p. 324.
2. According to Dr. Len Horowitz, the Rockefeller family has held a monopoly on American medicine since the 1920's. (Ref: *Mary Starrett Radio Show,* KPDQ, Portland, Oregon, 3/21/01.) Dr. Horowitz makes a similar point in "The American Red Double-Cross." (www.tetrahedron.org.) Dr. Horowitz states, "By 1907, medical education had been mostly monopolized by the Rockefeller consortium."

3. 90% of our food dollars in the U.S. are spent on processed foods. (Ref: Jeff Rense/*Sightings Radio Show,* KOTK, 3/16/01.) This fact is also stated in "The Real Reason We're Fat," by Gina Mallet, www.globeandmail.com, 11/4/06, p. F-7.

4. F. Batmanghelidj, M.D., *Your Body's Many Cries for Water* (Global Health Solutions, 1992) p. 115.

5. On the physical level, allergies and asthma are both associated with severe dehydration. (Ref: *Body's Many Cries for Water,* p. 120.)

6. McCabe, *Oxygen Therapies,* p. 82.

7. McCabe, *Oxygen Therapies,* p. 83.

8. McCabe, *Oxygen Therapies,* p. 82.

9. Dr. Hidemitsu Hayashi, *Microwater, the Natural Solution* (Water Institute, 1991). Information on high-pH water is taken from a two-page pamphlet, hereinafter called "Microwater brochure," that was condensed from an earlier brochure written by Dr. Hayashi located at www.xmission.com/~total/health/microh2o/welcome. For more details on Microwater, also see James Kahn's article, "Alakineionized Water: Living Water and Hunza Water." www.detoxifynow.com.

10. For additional information about H_2O_2, see *Oxygen Therapies,* by Ed McCabe.

11. Oxygen can be added to the system for improved health and energy. Dr. William Campbell Douglass advocates "exercising with oxygen." This is described in his booklet, *How to Slow Down the Aging Process,* available through Second Opinion Publishing, Box 467939, Atlanta, GA 31146.

12. McCabe, *Oxygen Therapies,* p. 84.

13. Dr. Keiichi Morishita, *The Hidden Truth of Cancer* (George Ohsawa Macrobiotic Foundation, 1972). Quote is from Microwater brochure. Also quoted on www.amazingwater.com.

14. Microwater US contact: Ion Light Company, 2263½, Sacramento, California 94115, 800-426-1110.

15. Hayashi, Microwater brochure.

16. It is estimated that an average of 894 cans of soft drinks are consumed each year per teenager. (Ref: Jeff Rense, *Sightings Radio Show*, KOTK, 3/16/01.)

17. 30 glasses of pH-10 water are required to neutralize a single 8-ounce soft drink. (Ref: Microwater brochure.) Dr. Batmanghelidj also talks about this problem in *Your Body's Many Cries for Water*, p. 104.

18. Dr. James Taylor, Ph.D., "Diet Drinks and Aspartame Disease." Quote was taken from a one-page flyer. For aspartame's fraudulent history see: www.mercola.com/article/aspartame/fraud.

19. Taylor, Aspartame article.

20. Batmanghelidj, *Body's Many Cries for Water*, title page and cover.

21. Hayashi, Microwater brochure.

22. Dr. Masaru Emoto, *Messages from Water*, (I.H.M. General Research Institute, Japan). Dr. Emoto's website: www.hado.net.

23. As the Earth changes its frequency, our cells are also experiencing an upgrade. Since our bodies are 70% water, hydrating with pure, high-quality spring water can greatly facilitate this shift. See www.SusanCreek.com, the author's website, for additional information about Enhanced Spring Water.

Chapter 9: Children of the Butterfly Paradigm

1. Bode, *Portable Thoreau,* p. 335.

2. Alice Bailey and Djwal Khul, *A Treatise on the Seven Rays, Volume 2: Esoteric Psychology II.* (Lucis Trust, 1942). The Piscean Age has been ruled by the 6th Cosmic Ray, the Ray of Devotion. While the positive aspects of this ray are devotion and service, the negative side produces dogma and fanaticism.

3. Allen, *Creating Wealth,* p. 291.

Chapter 10: 2012 and the Blue Star Prophecy

1. Moira Timms, *Beyond Prophecy and Predictions: Everyone's Guide to the Coming Changes* (Ballantine Books, New York, 1994) p. 245.
2. Scott Peterson, *Native American Prophecies* (Paragon House, Second Edition, 1999) p. 198.
3. Millie Moore, Talk transcript: "Living the Shariyat," ECKANKAR HI Retreat, 1999.
4. "Native American Prophecies: Tales of the End Times," *Body-Mind-Spirit Magazine,* Jan/Feb, 1993.
5. Weidner and Bridges, *Monument,* p. 184.
6. Sean David Morton, (Ref: *Coast to Coast with George Noorie* radio show, KEX, Portland, Oregon, 3/29/03.) Morton also writes about the Rand Corporation's findings on his website: www.delphiassociates.org/archive/Delphi_103.pdf.
7. Braden, *Isaiah Effect*, p. 54.
8. Carlos Barrios & Ludovica Squirri, *Kam Wuj: El Libro del Destino* (Editorial Sudamericana, 2002).
9. Braden, *Isaiah Effect*, p. 54.
10. Clow, *Pleiadian Agenda,* pp. 4-5, 49, 105.
11. Gilbert & Cotterell, *Mayan Prophecies,* p. 2.
12. Gilbert & Cotterell, *Mayan Prophecies,* inside jacket.
13. Braden, *Isaiah Effect*, p. 56.
14. Weidner & Bridges, *Monument,* p. 173.
15. Braden, *Isaiah Effect,* p. 66.
16. Timms, *Beyond Prophecy and Predictions,* pp. 159-160.
17. Timms, *Beyond Prophecy and Predictions,* pp. 160, 281-3 (several sentences combined).
18. Gordon-Michael Scallion, *Notes from the Cosmos* (Matrix Institute, 1987, 1997) pp. 203-211.
19. Braden, *Isaiah Effect,* p. 67.
20. Motorola is installing ELF cellular phone towers under a military contract in many parts of the United States. Reportedly these towers have

10,000 times more power than will be needed for cell phone use in the next 100 years. Related information on cell phone towers can be found at www.educate-yourself.org.

21. Speaking Wind's Millennium Prophecy: www.-energymedicineassn.com/speakingwind/news/1999.

22. According to Braden, historically the resonance frequency of Earth has been around 8 Hz. Now, at the close of the Piscean Age, the vibration is rapidly approaching 13 Hz. (Ref: *Awakening to Zero Point,* p. 31.)

23. Robert Ghost Wolf, *Days of Destiny,* excerpts from his website: www.wolflodge.org, 5-6-03.

24. Star Nation article: "Truth or Consequences," www.think-aboutit.com/native/prophecy_2.

25. Dr. Noel Huntley, "Self-Referencing Systems in the Relative Zero," April, 2004. See Dr. Huntley's website, *Duality and Beyond*: www.users.globalnet.co.uk/~noelh.

26. Weidner & Bridges, *Monument,* pp. 151-176.

27. Weidner & Bridges, *Monument,* pp. 9,12.

28. Weidner & Bridges, *Monument,* p. 239.

29. Weidner & Bridges, *Monument,* p. 173.

30. Weidner & Bridges, *Monument,* p. 239.

31. Weidner & Bridges, *Monument,* p. 174.

32. Icke, *Biggest Secret,* pp. 476-477.

33. Icke, *...and the truth shall set you free,* p. 483.

34. Clow, *Pleiadian Agenda,* p. 31.

35. Clow, *Pleiadian Agenda,* pp. 4, 31-33.

36. Clow, *Pleiadian Agenda,* p. 33.

37. Character: Andy Dufreine. Quote taken from the movie, *"The Shawshank Redemption,"* Columbia/Tri Star Pictures; Castlerock Entertainment (1994); adapted from a short story by Stephen King.

Chapter 11: In the Garden of the Gods

1. Paul Twitchell, *The Shariyat-Ki-Sugmad, Book I.* (Illuminated Way Press, Third Printing, 1972) pp. 19-20.
2. Twitchell, *Shariyat,* p. 20.
3. Paul Twitchell, *Stranger by the River* (Illuminated Way Press, Fifth Edition, 2003) p. 133.
4. Farid ud-Din Attar, *The Conference of the Birds* (Shamballa Publications, 1971) p. 129.
5. An audible form of symbolic communication. For more information see *The Secret Language of Waking Dreams,* by Michael Avery (ECKANKAR, 1992).
6. Reader's Digest, "The Flying Wallendas," circa 1979. A similar quote can be found on the Wallenda family website located at www.wallenda.com/history. "Life is being on the wire, everything else is just waiting."

Chapter 12: Somewhere Along the Way

1. Robert Frost, *The Poetry of Robert Frost, edited by Edward Lathem* (Henry Holt and Company, New York) p. 105.
2. Thomas Wolfe, *You Can't Go Home Again* (New York: Harper & Brothers, 1941) p. 706. Original quote reads, "You can't go back home to your family, back home to your childhood, back home to romantic love, back home to a young man's dreams of glory and of fame...back home to the father you have lost and are looking for, back home to someone who can help you, save you, ease the burden for you, back home to the old forms and systems of things which once seemed everlasting but which are changing all the time, back home to the escapes of Time and Memory."

Epilogue

1. Jack McCoy, verse from a song entitled "Master of Illusion," *Journey to the Heart* album, 1993 (song lyrics have been revised). Contact artist at: Mystic5751@aol.com.

INDEX

D

E

F

ABOUT THE AUTHOR

Michael Harrington grew up near Colliding Rivers in southern Oregon. He works as a water quality specialist in the Pacific Northwest where he has lived for the better part of his life. Besides writing, Michael enjoys softball, Alpine skiing, Tae Kwon Do, and hiking through old growth forests. His favorite trails lead to waterfalls strung out like jewels along the many tributaries of the scenic North Umpqua River. He relaxes by going for rides in the country with his Ragdoll cat, Jake. Michael generally drives.

*　　　　　*　　　　　*

Please visit www.SusanCreek.com
for author photo, information on water,
and other books by Michael Harrington.

Porcupines at the Dance
Parables and Stories from Colliding Rivers
by Michael Harrington

Porcupines at the Dance is loosely based on Michael Harrington's initial meeting and early conversations with John Redstone, the man he affectionately calls "the Chief." Set amongst old-growth forests and cascading streams, the Chief shares insights gleaned from the school of life with his new friend, a recent high school graduate about to enter college.

This prequel to *Touched by the Dragon's Breath* in the Colliding Rivers series features discourses on the Circle of Life, the secret name of God, giving and receiving, Soul's quest for love, the 7-Rays, and the twelve nidanas (of the Wheel of Life). Seated before the campfire each evening, the Chief illuminates points made during the day with colorful and thought-provoking stories reminiscent of Kahlil Gibran's, *The Wanderer*.

Highlights from their weeklong excursion, extending from Colliding Rivers to Horseheaven Creek, Mr. Redstone's spiritual home, include trips to an old prospector's cabin and a sacred Native American site, where the author experiences his first vision quest.

This fateful meeting at Colliding Rivers alters the boy's course in life, and enables the Chief to fulfill a promise made in a prior time when their roles were reversed.

*   *   *

ISBN#: 978-0-9748716-1-5
Price: $14.95 (188 pages)